Let in the Light

D1019739

Let in the Light

Facing the
hard stuff
with
hope

> "Pat Livingston opens our eyes to see the
> mystery of God right where we are."
> Henri J.M. Nouwen

Patricia H. Livingston

SORIN BOOKS   Notre Dame, Indiana

Unless otherwise indicated, Scripture texts used in this work are taken from the *New American Bible,* copyright © 1970 by the Confraternity of Christian Doctrine, Washington, DC, and are used by permission of the copyright owner. All rights reserved.

© 2006 by Patricia Livingston

All rights reserved. No part of this book may be used or reproduced in any manner whatsoever, except in the case of reprints in the context of reviews, without written permission from Ave Maria Press®, Inc., P.O. Box 428, Notre Dame, IN 46556.

www.sorinbooks.com

ISBN-10 1-933495-00-6

ISBN-13 978-1-933495-00-2

Cover and text design by Katherine Robinson Coleman

Printed and bound in the United States of America.

Library of Congress Cataloging-in-Publication Data

Livingston, Patricia H.
  Let in the light : facing the hard stuff with hope / Patricia H. Livingston.
        p. cm.
  Includes bibliographical references.
  ISBN-13: 978-1-933495-00-2 (pbk.)
  ISBN-10: 1-933495-00-6 (pbk.)
  1. Suffering—Religious aspects—Catholic Church. 2. Consolation. I. Title.

BX2373.S5L58 2006
248.8'6—dc22

To my sisters, Peggy and Mary,

beacons of light for me

in the mystery of darkness.

I am deeply grateful to my sisters and to all the others who were willing to share the light by giving permission for their stories to appear in these pages. In some cases, names and details have been altered for privacy.

Contents

Prologue: Too Much Dark

It was from George that I heard the best expression of my reason for writing this book. It was the first day of school and, in what can only be described as cruelty to both parents and teachers, school in that county began at 7:20 a.m. This meant getting up at 5:45. I had arrived the night before to help a bit with getting the gang off that first morning. George, at four years old, was very excited about being in preschool; "real school," he called it. Most uncharacteristically, he got right out of bed when his mom called him. He headed straight for the bathroom, but he missed the doorway and ran smack into the bedroom wall. George's "thump" was so loud, I heard it in the kitchen where I was starting breakfast. I thought he had fallen out of the top bunk. I came on the run, calling: "George, George, are you all right?" "I'm okay, Grandma," he replied slowly. "It's just…I guess…I have too much dark in my eyes." That phrase has stayed with me ever since. We live in a time when there is a great deal of dark in our eyes as a human family: terror and retaliation, war and scandal, epidemics and natural disaster. Political battles have turned venomous. Corporate immorality has left us in shock. And for many of us, there is darkness in our private lives—darkness that others know about and darkness that they do not. I am writing this book because there is too much dark in our eyes. We are badly bruised from running into the walls of our existence, trying to find a doorway. More clearly than at any other time in my life, I am aware of how important it is to let in the light. Life is an adventure of daunting difficulty, and we need all the light we can get. I want to pass on sources of illumination for me. As always when I write, I wish this were a conversation, and that you would pass yours on to me.

1

Light and Life

"I think," said Roscuro, "that the meaning of life is light."

Kate DiCamillo,
The Tale of Despereaux

Since I have had grandchildren, I have been reconnected with the childhood fear of the dark. Many times I have heard little voices call out, "*Please* leave the night light on!" with a kind of desperation, as if their lives depended on it.

Why do we have such a fear of the dark? Why is light such a significant source of imagery for our sense of life?

Why are the first words of creation in Genesis "Let there be light"?

Far more than just a metaphor, light is actually the primary source of physical life itself. My eyes were opened to this by cosmologist Brian Swimme. In his writing and speaking, he reminds us how utterly dependent we are on the light of the sun.

In an interview that appeared in *U.S. Catholic* magazine, Swimme explains:

> Our sun creates light by an amazing process where 600 million tons of hydrogen are transformed into 596 million tons of helium. The 4 million tons left over become light. Every second our sun is transforming 4 million tons of itself into light . . . the light disperses in all directions. Everything that's happened in the life of this planet is directly dependent upon that light. We're moving here and talking and thinking only because coursing through our bodies is the energy from the sun. If the sun were not there, earth's temperature would be 400 degrees below zero. The whole biosphere would shrivel up and die.[1]

In other words, all of human activity is powered by the generosity of the sun. It is this light, this outpouring gift of the sun from which life comes, that is a primary metaphor for God. "Light" and "God" are used interchangeably in the familiar phrases of the Nicene Creed: "God from God, light from light, true God from true God." In the Gospel of John, Jesus says, "I am the light of the world" (8:12). In the prologue the good news is summarized: "The light shines in the darkness and the darkness has not overcome it" (1:5).

In recent times the threat of darkness has become much more real. We are aware in deeper ways than ever how fragile life is. How vulnerable and permeable is our sense of safety. Our trust. Our hope.

There is a phrase that captures this for me. Years ago it was the title of a movie based on a novel by Czech author Milan Kundera. I remember it well because it was an excruciating experience for me at the time. I was teaching for a few days in a sabbatical program for priests held at St. Patrick Seminary in the Diocese of San Francisco.

At the end of my first day of teaching, an old friend invited me to see a movie. The friend is a priest on the faculty of the seminary, a highly respected scripture scholar and author, perhaps the most refined person I have ever met. He had read some good reviews of the film and was gathering a group to see it that evening.

What none of us had realized was that the film was highly erotic. It was not explicit in the way pornography is, but far too explicit for comfortable viewing for us together. The only similar experience of discomfort I can remember was when my sons took me to see *Fatal Attraction* at our local theater. It was Randy's idea—he thought I might like it because he knew I taught workshops in relationships. Boo came along.

I was sitting between them in the row, and if you ever saw that film you can imagine why Boo leaned over to Randy not long into it and said: "Sure, Randy, great movie to take MOM to, what in the world were you thinking?!!!"

I got a great chuckle out of it. All those years I tried to monitor what they watched, on TV or in the movies, and here they were telling me to close my eyes. Well, in the San Francisco art theater, sitting with this gentlest and holiest of priests, I squirmed more than my boys did in *Fatal Attraction.*

There was, however, a powerful message in the film, if I understood it. (I was never quite sure I did—a complex movie about sex and love and war.) I later told my friend that I thought somehow the message was in the title. Haunting to me, and enigmatic, it touched something very important about life.

The title of the movie is *The Unbearable Lightness of Being.*

The title poetically captures the exquisite fragility of life: the gossamer beauty held in being in *this* moment, in something as ephemeral as a rainbow or a soap bubble or the smile of a baby as it sleeps. In the miracle of each of us, just now, alive in the beating of our hearts.

All of it so delicate. The unbearable lightness of being.

How precious and fragile life is every moment. As we have seen in these last years, perhaps more than other times we can remember, it can be lost in a New York minute. Its innocence plundered, its trust betrayed, its hope swept away beneath tsunamis of sea or spirit.

We live on the margin in the unbearable lightness of being. Our glad lives are balanced on what novelist Reynolds Price calls "life's windswept tightropes,"[2] held by grace itself and only grace. I am convinced that no skill we ever learn is more important than throwing open every door and window in our hearts and minds and souls to that grace: embracing all the ways we can find of letting in the light.

2

The Power of Negativity

The cholesterol of the Spirit is negativity—
it clogs up the arteries of our souls. . . .
    Jill Biebel

Letting in the light—and by that, I mean thoughts, feelings, actions, experiences that create positive energy in us and those around us—can alter the course of things in ourselves and in our world. I have become increasingly convinced of this.

It has taken me a long time to realize that negativity has enormous power. Years ago I took a workshop to earn continuing education credits for my counseling license. I do not even remember what the subject of the course was, or who taught it. I do remember, however, the presenter's statement that negativity has the same intense power as violence and sex. At the time, I turned to a friend sitting next to me and said, "I don't agree with that."

But I paid attention in the days and months that followed and was totally won over. Negativity has great power.

One example is the feedback we get from other people. Psychologists say the ratio is twenty to one. In other words, it takes twenty compliments to offset one negative criticism. Originally, I doubted this—until I noticed how true it was in my own life.

Another example is negativity in the past that continues to have power. This is obviously true about significant experiences of trauma, but it also turns out to be true about minor happenings. Studies show that people remember things they got wrong on tests in the fifth grade, but remember nothing specific they got right!

People remember the basketball game they played when their foul shot did *not* go in just as the buzzer sounded more vividly than the games where their free throws scored.

I don't know how many dances I went to in high school and college; they are mostly a memory whirl of color and music and excitement. The one exception I can remember in perfect detail was the prom when my date called the night before to say he was taking someone else!

Negativity about the future can equally impact us. We can spend a great deal of time dreading things that never happen. Erma Bombeck often wrote about this: "I worry about introducing people and going blank when I get to my mother ... I worry about scientists discovering someday that lettuce has been fattening all along."[1] Psychologists say that over 90 percent of what we worry about never happens, yet those fears still have great strength.

Then there is negativity in the present; it can spoil our day. I am continually amazed at how irritated I can become by some small thing: someone zooming into the parking place I have been waiting for, someone playing loud music in the next apartment, someone eating what I had planned to use for dinner. Even the noises someone makes when they eat can eclipse my good feelings about them as a person at that moment! It is so humbling to notice how my irritation can take over my world.

I have also been paying attention to negativity in sports: A successful season can be totally altered by the first loss. Even if a football team makes it all the way to the Super Bowl, they are seen as losers as soon as they are not victorious in that final arena. Winning a silver medal at the Olympics is not enough; nothing seems to matter but the gold.

Another example I am struck by is the use of negative ads in political campaigns. These ads have proliferated exponentially. Everyone I know complains about them. News commentators bemoan them. And yet their use grows and grows, both in number and intensity. Why? Because they work! They have great power. When people go to vote, the negative attacks stick in their minds.

I am increasingly aware of the harmful force of many kinds of negativity: of gossip, of cynical remarks, of mockery. One person in a bad mood darkens a whole office staff or a whole family outing. I have been completely won over to the truth of the statement from that long-ago workshop: Negativity has the same intense power as violence and sex.

A related and very important learning for me is that negative thoughts affect us physically. Candace Pert at Georgetown University has done fascinating research, summarized in her book *Molecules of Emotion*.[2] She discovered that negative emotions—such as anger or resentment, or the fear that stalks us in these days of color-coded threat produce chemicals such as adrenaline, cortisol, and cyclophosomide that flood every cell of our bodies and cause stressful reactions.

Positive emotions, on the other hand, flood our cells with chemicals such as endorphins, interleukins, and interferons that produce relaxation and joy. Laboratory analysis reveals that tears of joy actually have a different chemical composition than tears of grief or rage.

Pert challenges us to choose carefully what we focus our thoughts on, because our thoughts produce emotions that quite literally affect the cells of our bodies.

It fascinates me to keep realizing that I can *choose* what I focus on, in a situation. It is easy for me to lose sight of this. The negative has great seductive power; in the midst of an experience, I can feel its magnetic pull. I have to remind myself that I have a choice, a choice made dramatically clear to me when I spent two nights in a hospital.

My daughter Kadee, at forty, had just given birth to her fourth child. The baby was born about 8:30 a.m., and the first hours were filled with enormous gratitude, relief, and joy. Tiny Daniel James was healthy and beautiful. Despite complications, Kadee had made it through her fourth Cesarean section well. Her husband John, the other grandparents, Daniel's three siblings, and lots of friends had gathered for the happy welcome.

By midafternoon it was time for some quiet. When John asked me if I would stay in the hospital with Kadee so he could look after the other children, I gladly agreed.

As the excitement of all the visitors faded, I began to find the hospital stay disturbing. What the marketing brochures had presented as "a bonding opportunity," I increasingly experienced as a seriously flawed system. According to the advertisement: "Everything happens in one cozy room: the labor, the birth, the stay of mother and baby."

I now realized what that meant, practically: There were no labor rooms, no delivery rooms, no separate maternity ward rooms, just one corridor for it all. Unless a woman had a C-section, it was all in the same place. There were women in labor up and down the corridor.

At one point, women in the rooms on either side of us were screaming. One poor woman was trying to deliver a fourteen-pound baby, another trying to deliver a baby who turned out to be breech.

All the nurses were focused on the emergencies. Of course, I understood this, but I tried for over an hour to get someone to come to our room when an alarm indicated that Kadee's IV fluid had run out.

It was twelve hours before anyone even checked her incision. When a nurse finally came in to look under the bandages, she was appalled that no one had examined the wound since morning. By this time Kadee had developed the crushing headache that is often the aftermath of the spinal punctures for the anesthesia. The nurse mumbled that someone should have warned her to lie flat.

With this "rooming-in" arrangement, it turned out that it was up to us to take full care of the baby: feed him, change him, treat his umbilical cord and record on a complex chart the exact amount of formula consumed and the color of the contents of the diapers.

What in the world did the mothers do who had no one to stay with them? I wondered. What if they fell getting in and out of these high beds? What if they got dizzy holding the baby? How did they even know what to do if this was their first baby?

Sometime around 2:00 a.m., as we were changing Daniel after a feeding, the power went out. Suddenly, our room was totally dark. After feeling my way to put the baby back in the bassinet, I ran out into the hall and questioned a nurse.

She said, "Don't make a fuss; this happens all the time."

"Happens all the time? The power goes out in the *hospital?*" my dumbfounded look must have communicated. She glared at me in the dim glow of the emergency power strip and walked away.

The power came back on after a while, but then at 4 a.m. the fire alarm went off. (I swear I am not making this up.) Again, I bolted off the cot, where I had been lying awake, and went into the corridor. "Just stay in the room!" the nurse yelled at me. "Stay in your room!"

"But if it is a fire, shouldn't we be getting the mothers and babies out of here?" I demanded.

"Don't make such a fuss! Go back into the room!" she shouted.

Eventually, the alarm shut off. In the lull we could hear again the ongoing chorus of crying newborns and groaning women in labor.

I tried to lie back down, but I could feel adrenaline pouring through my body. I just could not believe this place! I had heard about the crisis in medical care in hospitals. I had heard about the severe strain on overworked nurses. But how could a medical system do this to these women? How could they advertise this maternity design as if it were some kind of a beneficial upgrade?

In the midst of my incensed mental tirade, I heard Kadee's voice softly calling me: "Mom . . . come over here." She was holding Daniel, wrapped like a papoose in the hospital receiving blanket, his dark hair framing his darling round face.

"Look at him, Mom! Just look at him. Isn't he a miracle?" She smiled that smile of hers that warms the whole world. "Such a miracle!"

I will never forget the impact of that moment. It was a stopped-in-my-tracks challenge to where I chose to put my focus. All I had been seeing was the negative.

"Just look at him," she said again.

And there he was, that perfect little boy. Against all odds, our little miracle. Tears filled my eyes. This time, not tears of fear and outrage and disbelief, but tears of humbled joy. How could I lose the positive perspective of what mattered most? Even if the power went out, even with the impossibility of rest, even with the inadequate care hyped as doing us a favor—still, we had our *Daniel*!

We choose our focus, and it can make all the difference. In the middle of that night in a room on a maternity ward, it was as if the light of a different kind of power made its way into my heart.

3

The Power of Reframing

I like to use the example of someone who has
painful arthritis in his left knee. Instead of
complaining about that to everyone who will
listen, he will remind himself that he does
not have pain in his right knee, or right and
left ankle, or right and left shoulders and
elbows. In fact, his pain is limited to just one
knee! This is not some trick to hide the fact
of painful arthritis, it is the simple truth.

Demetrius Dumm, OSB,
Praying the Scriptures

It is no small thing, choosing to focus on life
instead of death, on hope instead of dread, on joy
instead of disillusion.

It matters, letting in the light.

23

In the dark of that hospital room the first night of Daniel James's life, I could feel the shift. As I looked at him with wonder, as I let my gratitude replace my fevered agitation, a change came to that room. Kadee smiled at me again and went to sleep at last.

There was a change in me, and in the room, in the place itself—even in the world.

This is what the quantum physicists are telling us. Our energy is very real. It makes a difference. It alters things. All living things are radically interconnected. In a now famous presentation entitled "Does the Flap of a Butterfly's Wings in Brazil Set Off a Tornado in Texas," meteorologist Edward Lorenz described it as the Butterfly Effect. Even the smallest of actions can make a big change.

It matters how we move our wings. This has become a crucial insight to me—so simple, but so central.

How we think affects what we see. We can choose what we focus our attention on. The classic example is that of a glass with water at a halfway mark. It can be considered either half-full or half-empty. I am humbled to realize that the "half-empty" perspective comes much more easily to me.

Changing what we choose to focus on, deliberately looking at a situation from another perspective, is a "reframe."

A favorite example I have quoted often comes from my friend Fr. Demetrius Dumm, a Benedictine scripture scholar. He speaks of David in the Bible as a man of hope. He describes David's reframe upon spotting the giant Goliath on the battlefield. Instead of saying, "He's so big, how can

I possibly defeat him?" David says, "He's so big, how can I possibly miss him? What a target!"

I have been working on reframes. Last week I was in a terrifying traffic situation just after dark. I was sitting in the back seat of a van coming home with friends from a dinner. We had exited the freeway and were driving down a four-lane road when I noticed a man up ahead walking across the street. He was in the middle of the road, not at an intersection or crossing of any kind, moving slowly, unevenly, sauntering along with a bottle of some kind in his hand. Drunk! I said to myself in a panic, realizing that my friend who was driving had not even noticed him.

"There's a man! A man in the road!" I yelled. The driver braked with all his might. At the squealing sound, the man looked up and then jumped into a sprint. We missed him by no more than two inches.

I sat there shaking, repeating silently inside myself, "We almost killed him, we almost killed him, we almost killed him." I could feel the chemicals produced by the terror pouring through me.

Wait a minute! I caught myself. Before saying anything out loud to my friends, I did a reframe. It took enormous effort, but somehow I pulled it off.

"We *missed* him! We missed him! He's *safe!*" I shouted.

"You're right!" said the driver who had pulled over to catch his breath. "He's safe! Holy Toledo! [not his actual words] He's safe!"

I could feel the energy in the car sprint from the energy of disaster to the energy of celebration. A reframe.

Sometimes we can shift to a positive view of something by reminding ourselves it could be worse. The phrase "At least it isn't . . . ." has been a help to me. When I am traveling, for example, and my flight is long delayed or canceled, I try to avoid sending my cells the chemicals that massive frustration produces by saying to myself, "At least I'm not traveling with toddlers." Years of trying to ride herd on small children in airports has given me that grateful perspective.

I have a friend who says, every time she gets sick or hurt in some way, "At least I don't have a kidney stone. . . ." Apparently, the intensity of kidney stone pain can dwarf all other health problems.

Recently, I saw two movies about World War II in France, vivid in their portrayal of the hardships of refugees fleeing Paris from the Nazi invasion. More than once since I saw the films, when I have been confronted with situations of significant uncertainty, I have consoled myself with a reframe: "At least I'm not fleeing Paris from the German army."

It sounds like such a small thing, maybe a silly mind game, but it really helps me. I can feel the butterfly wings flapping. I can sense something quite different in my body.

Another kind of reframe, or influence toward positive perspective, relates to our expectations. What we are expecting has a great influence on whether we view an experience as negative or positive.

The daughter of a friend of mine gave me a wonderful phrase for this. She was telling me about

a weekend away with her husband. They are
committed to hiring a baby-sitter every few months
and going away together somewhere for a couple of
days, just the two of them.

This particular time, there had been a lot of
stress leading up to their departure. They had been
snapping at each other, and resentment was thick
in the air of the car. Both of them began dreading
the weekend. They felt the pressure to be romantic,
but what they really felt was exhausted. They felt
constrained to be charming company, but what
they desperately needed was some quiet private
time in.

Since they were not even talking to each other
as they drove, Deb started to read a magazine. On
the third page was a cartoon that caught her
immediate attention. She laughed out loud and
showed it to Tom at the next light. That was the
turning point of the weekend.

I still have the cartoon she drew for me on a
napkin. A woman is sitting in a big chair reading a
book to a child in her lap. On the cover of the book,
the title is *Fairy Tales*. Across the bottom of the
cartoon is the sentence the woman is reading
aloud: "And they lowered their expectations, and
lived happily ever after. . . ."

"It saved us that weekend," Deb said, "lowering
our expectations. We began talking to each other
with the cartoon on the seat between us in the car.
We said things to each other such as, 'Let's just kick
back. Rest. Savor being off duty. We'll talk if we feel
like it, but if we don't, we'll just chill out. Read if we
want, watch TV, go for a walk. If we feel like doing
it together, fine. But no pressure. If we just want

room service pizza instead of dressing up for some fine restaurant, pizza it is.'"

She grinned, remembering. "We started to laugh at various ideas of how low our expectations could go. He said, 'What if I just watched football?' I answered 'What if I just read my book?' And that's what we did! All we did was sleep and read and watch TV. We had no meaningful conversation, did no planning for the future, made no important phone calls, did no shopping. It was exactly what we needed, as worn out as we both were. We held hands all the way home, deciding it was one of the best weekends we ever spent!"

Changing our expectations or reframing how we look at something can make a big difference in something as pleasant as a weekend away. In the crisis of a radical change in our health, it can be imperative.

As I am writing this book, someone I love very much is having to do an enormous reframe on her life. My sister Peggy, just twenty months older than I am, has something seriously wrong with her brain. About four years ago, those of us who love her began to notice that she had unmistakable difficulties with her memory. One doctor diagnosed it as Alzheimer's disease. Another suggested that it was late-onset symptoms from some earlier head injury. Her daughters call it "the brain thing."

Only with difficulty can Peggy now do many things that she had once been the best in the world at doing. Such as speaking. For decades she has been a gifted communicator—in intimate conversation, in meetings, in public speeches to big crowds. At least once a month she was on television in a local news network segment called "Young at Heart." Her profession involves working with and for those who are aging, and her television spots were updates or features for senior citizens. She would do these shows with no written notes, completely at ease, never missing a word.

With the progress of "the brain thing," she, who was flawlessly articulate, must wrestle with aphasia. She is hindered when searching for a word or phrase, forced to hesitate in midsentence.

Most of her life she could do four or five things at one time, never missing a beat. Now simple motor tasks, such as fastening a seat belt or buttoning a jacket, present frustrating challenges.

Finding her way has become problematic. She who got us around the city of Washington on public transportation when she was in the third grade, she who figured out the London underground when we were in college, now gets lost sometimes going to her doctor and has to go home again.

She has had to give up her job. She drives only in her neighborhood.

When it began to be clear that, whatever the diagnosis, her condition was not going away, she and I had a conversation. "I've got to find a way to think about this," she said, "a way to frame it so there is somehow room for hope."

This book is about finding room for hope. For Peggy, for me, for all of us.

Much of it may be familiar territory—from dealing with difficulties like health struggles, anxieties about loved ones, financial worries, significant losses, or fears that are seldom spoken out loud. But I am convinced that at this time in our private lives—and the life of the human family—we need to share any and every insight that helps us reframe darkness into light. We need to fan the flame of hope.

4

The Mixedness of Life

If you are on a road with no obstacles, it
probably doesn't lead anywhere.

Bumper sticker

Reframing a situation in a positive light is not
the same thing as pretending the negative is not
real. I have been greatly helped by a growing
acceptance of how inescapably mixed all life is:
glad happenings and bitter ones, good fortune and
bad.

Painful emotions are not optional, and it is
important not to bury those emotions in an attempt
to avoid negative thoughts. "All honest emotions are
healthy," Candace Pert assures us. "To repress
emotions (such as anger, fear and sadness) and not
let them flow freely is to set up a dis-integrity in the
system. The key is to express it and then let it go,
so it doesn't fester, or build, or escalate out of
control."[1]

We need to face the truth of the human condition: There is no way to avoid struggle and suffering, making mistakes, getting our hearts broken. As my son Randy said to his younger brother long ago when he was first attempting to master a two-wheeler in our driveway: "Face it, Boo. There's no way to learn to ride a bike without losing some skin."

As we ride through the mixedness of our years, we all lose a lot of skin. We need to learn to be at home with imperfection.

One place where I really enjoy the mix is in church. I appreciate the reverent tone of things, the solemnity of the sacred, but I also delight in the occasional humorous happening. A detour into the droll is, for me, a definite wink from God.

Sometimes lectors make mistakes. I appreciate these moments because they make me feel more at home with the mistakes I have made that week. Some words in scripture are harder to say than others. The letters of Paul to the Philippians can pose pronunciation problems. I have often heard "Paul's letter to the Philippines," but my favorite is one that composer David Haas reports hearing: "The second reading is taken from the letter of Paul to the Fallopians."

Students at our parish school are encouraged to attend 9:00 a.m. Mass with their families. The lectors are seventh- or eighth-graders. One Sunday the Old Testament reading was about the king of Babylon, Nebuchadnezzar. The way the boy said it was wonderful. He called him "King Ne buuk a dinosaur."

One of my favorite lector mistakes happened one time when the second reading was from the first letter of Paul to the Corinthians. Because Corinth was a wild seaport town famous for its practices of dissipation and debauchery, Paul was warning his congregation of new Christians against this. The passage begins, "The body . . . is not for immorality, but for the Lord" (6:13).

In the parish where I was visiting, however, what the lector said instead was, "The body is not for immortality. . . ."

A few sentences later, with great expression and conviction, looking around at all of us, riveting us with his wonderful, stern gaze he said, "Avoid immortality!"

I just loved that. Avoid immortality. As if we could!

Immortality is not optional. The mystery of the kingdom of God is that we are made for eternal life. We are born of God's great longing, and into God's arms we all return. The journey in between is a mixture, an ongoing amalgam of unfair losses and unexpected gifts, heartbreaking rejections and love out of nowhere. We all labor and are burdened, and we all are given rest.

We lose some skin learning to ride our bikes, but as we lose it, we come to know the central human wisdom: the perfection of imperfection.

In a lovely Christmas letter last year, summarizing the interweavings of her family's events, my friend Mary Kay Pasin wrote: "As I review the past year. . . . I am struck that the biggest news is that I have been given a gift of new awareness that is helping me in this ageing period of life. I have realized that I have viewed events of life as either negative or positive. The valuable awareness is that life is much more about 'both/and' than about 'either/or.'"

Sue Cosgrove, a friend in New Zealand, sent me the wonderful lyrics to Leonard Cohen's song "Anthem," which I have said over and over to myself:

Ring out the bells that still can ring,
Forget your perfect offering,
There is a crack in everything,
That's how the light gets in.[2]

This image of the light pouring through the cracks in our perfectly imperfect, mixed-up lives is a source of deep joy to me.

In the 2004 Newbery medal winner for children's literature, *The Tale of Despereaux*, I came across the wonderful word *chiaroscuro*. It is a combination of two Italian words, *chiaro* meaning clear and *oscuro* meaning dim. It is often used in describing a painting, such as Vermeer's *Girl With a Pearl Earring*, to point to the distribution and treatment of light and shade in a picture. In this story, Chiaroscuro is the name of a rat who, instead of loving the darkness of his home in the dungeon, loves the light instead. His very name means the arrangement of light and dark together.[3]

Chiaroscuro is the exact word I would use to describe a recent summer evening and all that was finalized then for our family. Whenever I think of that night, I see it as a painting, its chiaroscuro breathtakingly portraying what psychologist Jon

Kabat-Zinn calls "the poignant enormity of our life experience."[4]

We were saying good-bye to the family house. My three children and nine grandchildren had gathered for supper on the last night in the place that had been home for almost thirty-five years. We had moved there from Texas when Kadee had just finished first grade, before the boys were even in school. It was the house where they grew up, and after they were grown, it was where they came back for Christmas and birthdays.

Shortly after Randy and Silvia married, they bought the house from me, raised their boys there, and continued to offer it for many larger family gatherings.

This spring Randy found a beautiful piece of land out in the country, the kind of place where he had dreamed of moving one day. There was a trailer on it that needed lots of work but could be fixed up to live in until they could save enough to build a home. He put a For Sale sign in the yard of our old house, and someone called and offered the asking price for it that very night.

In June the real estate closing had been completed, and it was to be turned over to the new owners the next day. That last night we had come to have the final meal and to tell the stories.

Everyone from all three families was there. Squeals rose as the seven boys and two girls greeted each other, tiny Daniel adding his voice to the rest.

My youngest son, "Boo"—his sister's nickname from the day I first brought him home—took charge of the process of the telling, leading us together from room to room, inviting our memories. What we remembered was fascinating: old wallpaper and long-dead pets; tricks the kids played on baby-sitters; the historic sibling chase that put a hole in Kadee's bedroom door; jumping on beds until they *did* break, as I had warned at least a thousand times.

There were some sagas I had never heard before, to which I soon declared, "I don't think I need to know more about *that!*"

We remembered chicken pox and boyfriends calling at the window; raccoons we thought were burglars, and the time the toilet overflowed; the rattlesnake I killed on the doormat, and the Easter egg we did not find till August. We revisited homework at the dining room table, wrestling on the living room rug, and measurements moving up the broom closet door.

We looked out the window at the grapefruit tree in the backyard, planted from a seed by Boo in the first grade, now much taller than the house, bearing every year the sweetest fruit in the county.

We stopped in the kitchen, catching our breath, touching the old white-and-yellow Formica counters. It was as if we could see the cookies cooling and the biscuits just rolled out, gallon jugs of milk and turkeys waiting to be carved. A thousand, thousand meals cooked and eaten. Someone remembered the first stove that got hit one night by lightning, and the portable dishwasher that was so much trouble we almost never used it.

We paused by the doorway between the living room and the family room that had originally been a screened-in porch. There was a sliding glass door there once, and Randy had run through it one night, not realizing Kadee and Boo had pulled it shut. He needed several hundred stitches. As we stood there, Randy said, "Let's have a prayer."

We prayed in thanksgiving for all the graces of our years there. For so many adventures that had stretched and strengthened us, scarred and scared us, deepened us in life.

I looked around as we stood praying. I could see on the faces of these beautiful young people, Kadee and John, Randy and Silvia, Boo and Caroline, and I could tell that they were seeing it—the whole painting, the chiaroscuro of light and dark. They did not say out loud that they remembered when their father once had lived here. They did not mention other losses that had strained the peace. With raising children of their own, they understood that there had been broken bones and fevers, endless loads of laundry, terrors about money, nights when someone did not make it home till after dawn.

As we prayed, we sometimes swallowed hard. So much had happened here. This house had held us through it all.

We prayed in gratitude for all that life together, and then we prayed for those whose home it would be now when we were gone.

At last we ate. Pizza, of course, and birthday cake, for we were also celebrating my birthday.

Here is the best part of all: The cake was an ice-cream cake, and it had been kept in the refrigerator, the instructions being *not* to keep it in a freezer or it would be too hard to cut. When they got it out, it had melted! It was a layer of cake swimming in rich cream soup, the top still bright with roses and "Happy Birthday, Grandma."

They were distraught, but I was thrilled: "It's perfectly imperfect!" The melted cake was still quite delicious; just not, like all the rest of life, exactly what was planned.

We lit the sagging candles, laughed, and sang: to birth, to growth, to coming home and moving on; to the piercing chiaroscuro of our lives.

5

Titration

Ti-tra-tion *n. Chem.* "To determine the strength or concentration of the ingredients of a solution by adding measured amounts of a suitable reagent until the desired chemical reaction has been affected."

The Reader's Digest Great Encyclopedic Dictionary

Life is essentially mixed. There are difficult, painful, diminishing moments of darkness; and there are peaceful, joyful, strengthening moments of light. The question is, how can we open ourselves more to light?

My husband Howard's reminiscing about his college chemistry study of solutions gave me a new image at the heart of the dynamic of mixedness. He could not remember the exact chemical content of the liquids they used, but he has never forgotten one particular, dramatic experiment.

Each student had two beakers of liquid, one clear and one dark. They conducted the experiment by a process called *titration*: adding one liquid to the other, drop by drop, until the moment the desired chemical reaction happens.

Howard remembered adding a whole sequence of dark drops to the beaker of clear liquid with no discernable change in its appearance. "Now," said the chemistry professor, "add one more dark drop." When he did so, the entire beaker of clear liquid turned dark! One more drop turned the tide. A saturation point had been reached, and the whole solution changed.

"And now," said the professor, circulating among the desks with another container of the clear liquid, "take one more drop of the clear, add it to the dark solution, and see what happens." He had them all wait until each student had a dropper ready with the one new drop. "Together!" he said. And they all added the waiting clear drop.

One clear drop, and the whole dark beaker changed back again to clear!

I find this a powerful image. Our lives are very much like those beakers of liquid. At a certain point, the margin between dark and light is very narrow. We are balanced on the edge. One drop either way makes all the difference.

We were tragically reminded on September 11, 2001, of how narrow this margin is. I have a friend in New York whose son and daughter each had a former college roommate who worked for Cantor Fitzgerald in the World Trade Towers. The morning of September 11, her son's roommate went to work and was never seen again. Her daughter's roommate overslept and saw from a distance the towers fall.

The balance of the whole universe is as close as this. I was stunned to read something similar in an interview with Brian Swimme:

> Once we discovered the fact that the universe is expanding, Stephen Hawking asked the question, "How fast is it expanding, and what would happen if it were moving at a different rate?" What Hawking learned is that if the expansion had been just slightly slower, the universe would have expanded out and then collapsed back into a massive black hole. If the expansion had been slightly faster, the universe would have expanded out but it would not have been able to form galaxies or atoms. It would just be dust.
>
> Hawking then asked, "How much play is there between the two?" It turns out that if the expansion of the universe were 1 trillionth of 1 trillionth of 1 trillionth of 1 percent slower, it would have become a massive black hole. And if it had been 1 trillionth of 1 trillionth of 1 trillionth of 1 percent faster it would have been too fast to form galaxies, stars, planets, and life forms.[1]

This crucial balance—in a chemical solution and in the universe—helps me renew my commitment to letting in the light. I had an experience that has convinced me even further.

At an annual physical checkup, I reported some symptoms that I had been finding bothersome, but not really alarming. My doctor ordered an arterial sonogram to be done the next week. It indicated that my carotid artery on the right side was 60 percent to 80 percent blocked! The doctor was bewildered. He did not expect to see this condition in someone like me, a nonsmoker with low blood pressure, low cholesterol, no diabetes. I remember him saying, "There is so much we don't know yet about what affects arteries."

I began the daily aspirin he suggested and paid attention to my diet. I also consulted my friends Benni and Loni, who give workshops on the power of the absolute connection between our bodies and our minds. They told me about the statement in Louise Hay's book *You Can Heal Your Life:* "Arteries are the carriers of our joy."[2]

I have to say that I have no idea how Hay or others in this health field discover the connections between specific parts of the body and psychological and spiritual conditions. However, the moment I considered my arteries as carriers of my joy, I was struck by the fact that in the past year there had been an almost endless series of struggles and worries, losses and strain. Bleak was the word for whole stretches of that time.

Hay suggests repeating like a mantra an affirmation for the healing of arteries: "Joy is flowing though me with every beat of my heart." I truly have no idea how, or if, this kind of thing works, but I thought to myself: "How can it hurt? What have I got to lose?"

I said the joy mantra, not at a regular time each day exactly, but whenever I remembered, especially at times when I began to feel worried or resentful or frustrated. I would focus on something for which I was deeply grateful and say to myself, "Joy is flowing through me with every beat of my heart."

I was surprised at how often this would snap me out of an encroaching funk. I was not sure what it was doing physically, but it was making me better company, especially for myself. I became aware that often, if something irritated me, it would be like the one drop that turned the whole solution dark.

I would begin frowning, inside if not outside. Then, if I remembered to start the mantra—or chose to do it if I remembered (sometimes I would need to just keep venting)—the amazing thing was that joy *would* start flowing through me! Like the experiment, the chemistry of my mood would reverse. A drop of light changed the balance.

I am not saying this always worked or was some kind of magic for times of significant difficulty, but I became convinced that it definitely made a difference.

My doctor had scheduled me for a six-month follow-up sonogram of my neck and brain. The results were fascinating: There was a very significant reduction in the carotid artery buildup!

Was it the mantra? Was it the aspirin every day? Was it the reduced intake of Ben and Jerry's ice cream? There is no way I could say for sure. As my doctor said, "There is so much we don't know about what affects arteries."

I believe the joy mantra helped. As Candace Pert's research suggests, I think the joyful thoughts changed my chemistry enough to make a difference. It certainly helped my sense of life.

Sometimes this titration trick does not happen because we choose to refocus. Sometimes events or energies themselves pile up, and then one more thing makes all the difference, as in the proverbial straw that broke the camel's back.

One small happening can also be the thing that *heals* the camel's back.

I have seen this kind of shift when someone in traffic is in a great hurry but is stuck trying to get out of a side street, trying to turn into the flow of backed-up traffic. If no one lets him in, through one signal light change after another, eventually he furiously tries to block the flow, perhaps giving people who honk the finger.

But if someone pauses and smiles while motioning him into the flow, a shift happens. Two blocks down, *he* is the one who pauses to let a car come into the lane.

A few years ago, I saw a fascinating shift in energy in a hotel in Bavaria where I was giving a retreat for the Military Council of Catholic Women. The council is an organization of women connected with the military in some way who meet regularly to deepen their spirituality. They had flown me from the United States to Germany to give the annual retreat, which was held in a big resort hotel. I realized early that there were two big groups in the hotel that weekend: our women and many German men who were partying for Octoberfest.

The women were extremely devout and met often to pray. The vacations they talked about at meals were not to luxurious hotels in famous cities, but to Lourdes or other pilgrimage shrines in Europe. Spirituality was a central focus of their lives.

The men had been drinking for days and seemed to be on the prowl for partying partners. I had seen some of them wandering the hallways either nude or with only the briefest of briefs, knocking on doors, loudly laughing.

The first night of the retreat, a group of the men were standing outside the disco in studly postures, beer in hand, when our women gathered in the hallway. The men lit up like Times Square to see these lovely young American women. They were secretly giving each other high fives. "All right . . . what a party!"

One ventured out to the blonde leader of our group saying, "You are here for the dancing, yah?"

"Oh *nein, nein,*" she said. "For the Rosary."

In the open, first-floor space on the other side of the lobby from the disco, the women were preparing to do the Living Rosary. Each of us had a candle representing a bead, and we were going to take turns saying the prayers aloud.

I thought the man was going to cry. "The Rosary! *Gott in Himmel!*" he said.

"God bless you too," she said, and smiled like Bernadette herself.

I wish I had a picture of his face. I was still laughing to myself at the end of the first decade of our prayers. Something made me look up, and I realized that we were on the floor of an atrium that formed the center of the hotel. The rooms on the ten floors above us were built in a square around the opening. On every floor people were lining the railings looking down on our living rosary. Suddenly I realized that many of them were actually saying the prayers with us!

A shift in the solution of the energy of that hotel had occurred. At least for that moment, the raucous spirit of an orgy had gentled into something touched by Mystery. On that night a drop of dignity and wonder was slipped into the party by these praying women—a blessing on the realm.

6

Dark Night of the Soul

Whenever I find myself in the cellar of affliction, I always look about for the wine.
Samuel Rutherford,
Seventeenth-century Scottish minister

One of the great blessings for me in growing older is that I have lived through—all the way through—significant times of darkness. I have been graced to discover totally unexpected gifts in the midst of what seemed to be only loss or turmoil, rare vintage wine for the soul in the "cellar of affliction."

This, it seems, is the truth at the heart of St. John of the Cross's concept of the Dark Night of the Soul. I must admit that, for many years, I was repelled by his concept. I avoided reading him or books about him, shuddering at stories I heard of his life, including accounts of beatings and imprisonment by his own Carmelite brothers. I am very uncomfortable with some of the practices of the great saints that seem to imply God is pleased with suffering. I did not want even to *hear* about the Dark Night of the Soul, let alone to experience it.

A friend sent me a tape of a talk by Gerald May, who was Senior Fellow in Contemplative Theology and Psychology at Shalem Institute, on the Dark Night of the Soul.[1] May said that what is given to us in our experience of the Dark Night is the illumination of God's love that can only come in the darkness.

He also explained that John of the Cross did not view the Dark Night necessarily as terrible, tragic darkness. The words for Dark Night in Spanish are *Noce Oscura. Oscura* means dim or obscure. To John, the darkness was one of confusion, unknowing, an obscuring of the way things were; a sense that something needs to be fixed, but no idea how. It is the darkness we experience when the way we are running things stops working, when things fall apart and we know we are not in control. There is a sense of loss of the way things were, and we are forced to admit that we *don't* know what should happen next.

It is at this point "of knowing that we don't know," May stated gently, "that the potential of letting God guide is born....The illumination is that God is at work, the secret work of the soul."

I love Gerald May's shorthand for the Dark Night of the Soul. He said it means "things are 'obscure for sure' or 'for sure obscure,' however you want to say it, that's how you know you are in it." In the obscurity there comes some kind of illumination of God's love. May quoted John of the Cross: "The Dark Night is about nothing other than Love. . . . "

I am grateful for this affectionate description of the Dark Night of the Soul. After listening to May, I began connecting it with a phenomenon very familiar to me, something I call the blessing in the mess.

It is something I have come to recognize more and more in life. Over time, it begins to be clear that life is messy, so much more so than we ever expected—and certainly ever wanted. And then in the very messiness, blessing often comes. "The illumination of Love," John might have said.

A great biblical theme, frequently underlined by scripture scholar Carroll Stuhlmueller, is that God creates out of chaos, brings life out of what seems to us like death. When everything is "obscure for sure," transformation may be near.

Creation out of chaos is the central theme of my book, *This Blessed Mess*. Since its publication, many people have shared with me powerful examples of this dynamic in their lives. When people tell me their stories, I feel as if I have been given a great treasure, another confirmation that God writes straight with crooked lines, as the old saying goes; that the Dark Night is about illumination and not about tormented testing. I am very grateful for these stories. Two special examples show different kinds of blessing that can come out of the mess.

One kind of blessing is *external*. Something comes out of the chaos, some kind of breakthrough, some new direction or outcome that never would have happened without the difficulty.

In Florida where I live, it is highly prudent to have an annual check and service of the air-conditioning unit. Each summer I make an appointment with Frank, the man who originally installed the unit. This particular year, the first thing he said when he came was, "How's your book coming?"

I laughed, realizing I must have been working on it every summer he was there for the last four years. I said, "You'll never believe it; it's going to be released in a couple of weeks."

"That's great," he said, "I can't wait to see it. People need your message."

"My message?" I asked, touched, but bewildered by his comment.

"Absolutely," he replied. "Isn't your book about creation out of chaos?"

"Why, yes, it is," I said, amazed that he not only remembered I was writing a book but also remembered what it was about!

"Has that been your experience, Frank?"

"It is the story of my life."

"Would you be willing to tell me about it?"

He told this story: "When I was seven, I became an orphan. My mother had died when I was five and then my Dad two years later. We lived in the mountains of West Virginia. There were nineteen of us kids. We younger ones were sent to an orphanage in Sevierville, Tennessee, in the Smoky Mountains. I thought it was the end of the world.

"But at the orphanage we *each* had our own bed. We'd never slept less than three to a bed before. Every day we had enough to eat—*three* times a day we had enough to eat. If we did our homework, there were basketball hoops and a baseball diamond.

"And clothes! People from churches sent us clothes—we were some of the best-dressed kids in school. People were poor in those mountains, some of the kids had clothes that were mostly in patches."

He paused, remembering, then said, "One girl I sometimes sat next to in my homeroom at school had lots of clothes with patches. She even wrote a song about patches. She grew up to be kind of a famous singer, and that song was a big hit. You might have heard of her. Her name is Dolly Parton."

"Dolly Parton! Yes, Frank," I said, shaking my head and smiling, "I've definitely heard of Dolly Parton! I know her song about patches."

He was quiet for a minute, thoughtful, then continued, "You know, going to that orphanage made all the difference. We knew we were cared about, and we could stay in school till we finished. They put it in our heads that we could make something of ourselves if we worked hard.

"Well, I have worked hard, and I have been able to make something of myself. I've had this little appliance business for years now, and it does fine. It was a terrible thing being an orphan at seven. But blessings came out of it. People need to know that can happen. I'm glad you wrote your book."

Frank's story is a great gift to me: the blessing in the mess, a whole new direction for a life, chaos as the raw material for creation.

The second story is about *internal* blessing. Going through chaos forces us to grow. It is as if we are driven into the desert, challenged to deepen, to look again at what life is really all about.

A friend of mine asked me to sign a copy of my book for another doctor at her hospital. Before I began to write an inscription, she gave me the background. The other doctor had a family practice in their western city and also appeared regularly on television, sought out as a commentator by the local TV station. She was able to explain complex medical issues very clearly, and she was strikingly beautiful. She had come to the attention of national networks and had been offered a lucrative contract to appear regularly on a famous weekly news program. It looked like the beginning of an exciting career direction.

The week after she accepted the offer, she was visiting her sister, and during the evening they had a very heated discussion about something. They were not at all angry with each other personally; they just loved to argue and debate issues.

The sister had a new dog, a large rottwieler, who became very upset by their exchange. He thought his mistress was being threatened by the strange visitor, and without even a warning growl, he leapt up and bit the doctor in the face. By the time they could get the dog to let go, she had terrible wounds.

The wounds healed, but even after plastic surgery, they left disfiguring scars and permanent nerve damage that make television appearances unlikely.

A few weeks after I signed the book for her, I received a letter saying she had felt compelled to write to thank me for helping her name the mystery of her own life. The injury was actually a source of real grace and wisdom. It helped her see what really mattered. A quarter of an inch over on her cheek, and she would have lost her eye. Half an inch over on her neck, and her carotid artery would have been punctured and she might have bled to death before she could get to the hospital. That she is alive and can see is a great grace. There is light for her on a possible new direction of her life.

"As strange as it sounds," she wrote, "in it's way it was a blessing."

I held her letter in my hand for a long time in silence.

Victor Frankl, who survived the Holocaust to write one of the most important books of the twentieth century, *Man's Search for Meaning*, wrote, "What is to give light must endure burning."

Jesus told us that to gain our life we must lose it. In the losing, a kind of dark night falls on the world as we have known it. Life becomes "obscure for sure." What can happen in the dark night, as these stories testify, is "the illumination of Love."

7

Sources of Light

There must be fire on the mountain . . . fire under the stone, fire over the sea. Fire to burn away the dark, for the Dark, the Dark is Rising!

Susan Cooper,
The Dark is Rising

As convinced as we may be that there are blessings in the mess, when hard times come again, everything in us recoils. Another round of turmoil is totally unwelcome. No one I know greets chaos saying, "Oh good, another chance for new creation!" When night moves in without a warning, we reach out desperately for light. We want fire on the mountain when the dark begins to rise.

Where can we find sources of light?

For many of us, the primary source of light is a core belief in God. In the aftermath of the terrible tsunami of December 26, 2004, I was deeply moved by demonstrations of this truth. Near the coast of Mahabalipuram, India, the enormous force of the wave removed sand deposits, uncovering structures of what appears to have been a seventh-century port city long submerged by the sea. Near the temple wall the receding waters revealed elaborately carved rock figures of a reclining lion, a horse in flight, the head of an elephant—animals somehow connected to ancient worship. This image has stayed with me as a metaphor of how the storms of human life can help uncover the rock of our belief.

In the stunning stories of tsunami survivors, different religious organizations were reported as lifelines for people trying to hold on to the light. When all the inhabitants of the primarily Christian Pillowpanja island off the coast of India were washed away by the giant wave, only Michael Mangal, a forty-year-old coconut farmer, was thrown back on land alive. He survived twenty-five days alone before being rescued by a boat. What helped him, he said, was reading the Bible he found in the rubble and praying.

When the parents of Baby 81, the infant boy found among debris and corpses left by the tsunami in Sri Lanka, were finally reunited with him after DNA testing proved he was their son, they offered temple sacrifices in gratitude to their Hindu gods, whom they believe brought about their son's recovery.

Ari Afrizal, a twenty-one-year-old carpenter, lived for two weeks adrift in the Indian Ocean, first floating on pieces of wood, then on a broken boat, and finally on a raft carrying a life-saving treasure of bottled water. Through all fifteen days in the terrible cold nights and the scorching days, he prayed in his Malay language to Allah for life. "I never got angry," he said after his rescue. "I was grateful to be alive. The heat comes from God. The cold comes from God. Death and life also come from God."[1]

While belief in God is a primary source of light, for most people there are other sources as well. Ari Afrizal talked about other things that helped him survive those days at sea. There was solace, he said, in nature's beauty, watching the simultaneous sunset and moonrise over the water. He thought of his parents, his two elder brothers, a younger brother and sister, his girlfriend. He thought of his special soccer teams, Manchester United and Real Madrid. He replayed scenes from his favorite Indian movies.

I am convinced that for each one of us there are particular sources of light that make a difference, some as profound as religious belief, some as simple as a soccer game or a movie. It is worth reflecting on what these sources are for us, worth consciously putting ourselves in the presence of light.

Places can be a source of light. All sorts of places. A favorite example for me comes from Audrey Hepburn's film character Holly Golightly. When Holly had "the Mean Reds," which was her term for the darkness, she would pick up coffee and a roll and stand looking in the jewelry store window and have breakfast at Tiffany's—her place of light.

A place that holds light for me is the Franciscan Center in Tampa, a retreat house on the

Hillsborough River, a place of such inspiration and hospitality that it is like a home for hope. Once, when a great storm threatened our city, one of the Franciscan sisters left a message on our voice mail saying that if our part of the city were to be evacuated, there would always be a room for us at the center.

Another such place of light for me is the bar at Armani's restaurant on top of a hotel near the airport. There you can watch the sun set over the bay, listen to piano music, and order anything you want from the four-star menu. Joan and John, who work there, welcome us like old friends with their expert, thoughtful, upbeat service. There is no need to have five courses, as you would in the restaurant itself; my husband and I usually have an appetizer and dessert. Savoring the food, music, and conversation, sipping wine or cappuccino, watching the sun's last colors play off the huge expanse of water and sky, a kind of deep illumination happens inside us.

Even when we are not in a special place, music by itself can brighten our world. I am fascinated by how many songs are about light. The ageless Sunday school song "This Little Light of Mine"; old classics such as "Shine On, Shine On Harvest Moon" or "You Are My Sunshine, My Only Sunshine"; the Beatles favorite, "Here Comes the Sun"; Debbie Boone's big hit, "You Light Up My Life"; Johnny Nash's "I Can See Clearly Now" ("The rain is gone . . . it's gonna be a bright, bright sunshiny day"). Perhaps my favorite is the 5th Dimension's chorus at the end of "Aquarius": "Let the sun shine in."

In recent weeks I watched two PBS fund-raising shows, one with music from the 1950s, the other with music from the '60s and '70s. For the occasion they brought back many of the performers who had recorded the original music. Watching them sing, white-haired and lined but totally alive, voices strong, moving with the beat, and seeing the audience singing with them, clapping, whistling, jumping to their feet in ovation after ovation, was thrilling to me. The power of those fine familiar songs shared together once again kindled a great glow.

Just as singing old songs can brighten life for us, I have noticed that repeating certain sayings can sometimes push back the shadows in hard moments. Sayings like the one from my favorite childhood story, *The Little Engine That Could.* Repeating "I think I can, I think I can, I think I can" kept the little engine moving heavy cars along the track. When I repeat that phrase, I am surprised at how much it helps me get something done.

My daughter Kadee has a kinship with animals and birds that gives her vivid images and sayings. When I am struggling, she sometimes says, "Mom, flap your wings, flap your wings! Say to yourself, 'I'm soaring, I'm soaring!'" It amazes me how that can pull me out of a downward slide. Telling myself I am soaring actually lifts my spirits sometimes enough for me to get a second wind.

Long ago Julian of Norwich, contemporary of Plantagenet kings, in a century wracked with war and plague, was given a refrain in one of her visions of Christ: "All shall be well, and all shall be well, and all manner of thing shall be well."

This is like the saying of Sharon, my sister Peggy's friend who worked in the office with her for years. Sharon is an extraordinary woman who has been a source of strength for family and friends through various sieges of difficulty. When something terrible happens, or someone is upset or hurt, she says in a tone that conveys deep caring, "It'll be all right, it'll be all right." With the rich texture of her Tennessee cadence, the sound is more like "It'll be all *raaht.*"

There is something profoundly comforting and hope-filled in the way she says it, the farthest thing from some offhand platitude. It has the sound of hope hard-won, surviving many troubles. On dark days Peggy repeats it to herself in Sharon's accent: "It'll be all raaht." As she says it, light comes in.

I have a new phrase that offers me a sparkle when I need it these days. It came from a card game I played with Kadee's older boys, first- and second-graders Johnny and Forrest. It was a game I never knew before, a simple game involving slapping your hand on a pile of cards when a match occurs. If you slap first, the pile is yours. You can imagine this has as much potential for horseplay as for skill, especially when the boys are in high gear.

When my cards would dwindle and come close to running out, they would hand me some of their cards so I would still be in the game. Whenever I would spot the match and slap and win the pile, they were absolutely gleeful. "Go, go, Grandma, go!" they started chanting every time I won a round. "Go, go, Grandma, go!" Pumping fists into the air.

More than once since that game, when I have felt myself sinking into worry, I have replayed their cheering from the sideline. It makes me grin. "Go, go, Grandma, go!"

Repeating refrains can help hold onto light.

Perhaps my favorite source of light is stories. I especially prize stories of narrow escapes, against all odds, in the nick of time. When I am living on the margin, they help me remember times when, in the end, things really were "all raaht." When the precipice seems near, I tell myself these stories and they let in the light.

It was October when my husband was driving the hundred-mile route home from a birthday party for our grandson Forrest. He was on an empty country road and going very fast. The only warning was a shifting motion he saw out of the corner of his eye in a clump of palmettos. Then there was an impact like a rifle shot. The windshield shattered, and the car filled with blood and flesh and feathers. A wild turkey had come through the windshield and splattered all over the inside of the rear window.

The bird broke through on the *passenger* side. If it had flown out a fraction sooner, it would have come through just in front of the steering wheel, and Howard would have been dead. If I had been sitting in the passenger seat, I would have been dead.

It was the first family birthday party I had ever missed. I was in Germany, giving the retreat for the Military Council of Catholic Women during Octoberfest. Before I flew to Frankfurt, I had talked to Forrest about missing his party, and he had hugged me and told me not to feel bad, that it was fine. How fine it really was, none of us knew till then! A narrow escape.

Here's a nick-of-time story I love. I was visiting my sister Peggy in Knoxville at the time of the University of Tennessee Law School Awards Banquet. Her husband Dick, a professor and former dean of the law school, invited us to go with them. "A command performance for us faculty," he said. "I've got to go, but your company would sure improve the evening if you are up to it. I must warn you, these events are lively, but they are very long. Awards in every subject, in every facet of law school life. Three hours, maybe, unless they keep them really clipping along."

We agreed to go. We sat at a table with six or seven students, all of whom had been in class with Dick at one time or another. He was proud of them and led us in a spirited conversation over dinner before the ceremony started. Then the awards commenced, and they did seem almost endless. The most fun occurred each time one of the students at our table was called forth. We cheered and clapped resoundingly and high-fived them when they returned.

Finally, the student awards were over, and the master of ceremonies began to give awards for service in the community or state to former students or others associated with the school. Many of the honorees were not present at the dinner. The energy was flagging.

Dick looked at his watch and motioned for us to lean over to his whisper: "I have a plan to beat the crowd," he said. "We can slip down the stairs behind us as if we were going to the restroom. Then we can go up another stairway—I spotted it when we came in—right by our coats. Out the side door and to the parking lot, we'll be the first ones out. Escape the crush!" His eyes were sparkling with the plan.

"Fine," we said. "Just give the signal and we're with you."

He did not move right then; he paused, and his hesitation took us past the moment when our departure would be masked by the sound of the applause. And then good manners caught him. It was too late for us to rise as the dean began the final item on his list. The perfect timing for our bolt had passed.

"This is a new award, one that has never been given before in the history of the school. It is given to a person who has contributed more than any other to the development of this Law School." He went on to describe courses taught, new ones created, clinics set up to help the poor, awards voted on by the students, a brilliant deanship during which a new law school was built, a Fulbright professorship in eastern Europe during a sabbatical. The list went on and on.

Dick sat unmoving, stunned. There was only one person this could be.

"And so, it is my very great honor to present tonight the first Lifetime Achievement Award at the University of Tennessee Law School to Richard Stanley Wirtz."

I heard a great intake of breath from Dick just as the students throughout the room leaped to their feet. They had not risen for any other honor. Cheering, applauding in great thunderous waves, they rose. Dick walked through them to the stage and accepted the award. The applause went on long after he sat down again.

Lifetime Achievement Award. We nearly missed it! Half a minute, maybe less, and we would have been in the basement heading for our coats.

This story holds the light for me. As I sketch in these pages some of what illuminates my journey, I am hoping you are reminded of sources of your own. Each of us responds to different forms of encouragement, but letting the light in can encourage us all.

8

Laughter

"The charm that repels a Boggart [a terrifying spectre that takes the shape of everyone's worst fear] is simple, yet it requires force of mind. You see, the thing that finishes a Boggart is *laughter*. What you need to do is force it to assume a shape you find amusing! We will practice the charm together without wands first. After me, please . . . *riddikulus!*"

J. K. Rowling,
Harry Potter and the Prisoner of Azkaban

Laughter is a marvelous source of light. A sense of humor is not something extra or frivolous, but a powerful iridescence that can hold off the dark.

I was delighted when I saw the film *Harry Potter and the Prisoner of Azkaban* that in the Defense Against the Dark Arts class, Professor Lupin teaches Harry and the other students to picture what they are most afraid of as something amusing, and to make the source of terror disappear by using the magic word "Riddikulus!"

Laughter can rout our fears. Norman Cousins' studies show that it can actually heal us, that laughter is truly the best medicine.

From the perspective of biophysics, medical and spiritual leader Dr. Depak Chopra shows that it is not just the content, the humorous thoughts that strike us funny, that have such a positive effect on us, but the very *sound* of laughter.

Sounds of all kinds cause the fluid in our cells to vibrate. Some frequencies and patterns are healing, some are destructive. The sound of laughter produces very healing vibrations. Something in us loosens up and lets go. The sound itself is healing. Chopra tells of groups in India who line up opposite one another and just start to laugh. There is no verbal content; people just start to make laughing sounds. Pretty soon the contagion takes over, and everyone is pulled into the laughter until they are bubbling over with crescendos of mirth. This goes on for twenty minutes or longer, then people go their way feeling lightened and energized.[1]

A woman who runs an assisted-living facility told me that she does this exercise with her resident men and women, and they delight in it. On days she forgets to invite them to line up, someone will confront her: "Sister! You didn't have us laugh!"

Laughter is a sound that has a universal wave length. I remember a *Family Circus* cartoon in which the little boy is watching his dad and a heavily bearded man dressed in clothes of a very

different culture. The two men are laughing at
something. The little boy says, "When he laughs, he
doesn't have a foreign accent!" Laughter is our
common human sound.

In the *National Catholic Reporter* there was a
fascinating article by Rich Heffern on Navajo
spirituality in which he quotes from a conversation
with Sr. Gloria Davis reflecting on her native Navajo
tradition. She explains that the holy ones in their
community, the ones who were the spiritual
leaders, "were always the people with the keenest
sense of humor. You could spot them by the laugh
wrinkles near their eyes!"[2]

In the same article, Lori Alviso Alvord, a Navajo
physician, explains, "After a Navajo baby is born,
the first celebration takes place just after the child's
first laugh. Yes, laugh! We believe the soul (also
called 'the wind') enters the body soon after birth.
A baby's laugh is an indication that the soul has
become attached to the body. The person who
made the baby laugh is expected to host a
party. . . ."

With nine grandchildren aged ten and under, I
have rediscovered the primal experience of
laughter. I had forgotten that there is a definite
stage when kids begin to tell jokes. It seems to be
sometime around the age of four. It is so hilarious!
They do not understand that the content of a joke
is meant to be funny. They have no idea there
needs to be a connection of some kind between the
parts. This is how it goes for them: After
announcing that you have a joke, first you say
something, then you say something else, and then
everyone laughs.

"Knock, knock" jokes are a perfect example. One child will say, "I've got a joke!" (Everybody listens— it is amazing how much attention that announcement can evoke from a group of children.) She continues: "Knock knock." They reply, "Who's there?" She says, "Orange." They answer, "Orange who?" She says, "Orange you going to let me in?" They all laugh.

Immediately, someone else says, "I've got one! I've got one! Knock, knock." "Who's there?" "Thea." "Thea who?" "Thea later alligator." And they laugh harder.

And then someone, probably the littlest one, shouts, "It's my turn, it's my turn!" He takes a deep breath. "Knock, knock." "Who's there?" "Alligator." "Alligator who?" "Alligator's eating the oranges!" And at that, they all totally crack up, laughing so hard they fall down. There is no comic content whatsoever, but at that joke they laugh the hardest of all.

The content is not nearly as important as the laughter itself. This was lucky for my mom, who never successfully completed a joke. But when she would even *start* to tell one, we would all rock with laughter. It was as if light came streaming into the room.

Much of the content of humor involves a reversal of some kind, a surprising new way of looking at or hearing what we have been used to, often a reversal involving a play on words, using the words in a different sense.

One of my favorite jokes came in one of those endlessly forwarded e-mails:

The Japanese eat very little fat and suffer fewer heart attacks than the British or Americans.

The French eat a lot of fat and also suffer fewer heart attacks than the British or Americans.

The Chinese drink very little red wine and suffer fewer heart attacks than the British or Americans.

The Italians drink excessive amounts of red wine and also suffer fewer heart attacks than the British or Americans.

Conclusion: Eat and drink what you like. It's speaking English that will kill you.

We laugh at shifts in the way we use the words or think of reality. We laugh at the improbable recombinations. We laugh when things get reversed, when what we expect is turned upside down, when we see or hear something in a whole new way. I love connecting this with the truth at the heart of Christian revelation, the greatest of all reversals: God became human and death became life.

Eugene O'Neill wrote a play called *Lazarus Laughed* that captures this reversal and names for me the central source of light. After Jesus left Lazarus's open tomb, family and friends were discussing the miracle of Lazarus's resurrection. Lazarus's wife, Miriam, told them that Jesus called out, "Lazarus, come forth!" A guest reported that Lazarus appeared in the opening of the tomb wrapped in his shroud.

The guest went on to say,

"I helped to pry away the stone so I was right
beside him. I found myself kneeling, but
between my fingers I watched Jesus and
Lazarus. Jesus looked into his face for what
seemed a long time and suddenly Lazarus
said 'Yes' as if he were answering a question
in Jesus' eyes. . . . Then Jesus smiled . . . and
Lazarus . . . began to laugh softly like a man
in love with God! Such a laugh I never heard!
It made my ears drunk! It was like wine! And
though I was half-dead with fright I found
myself laughing, too!"

Then Lazarus, who had been lying still, stood up
and said in exaltation, "There is no death . . . there is
only life! . . . there is only laughter! . . . and I laughed
in the laughter of God."[3]

Laughter lets in the light. Dead seriousness
surrenders to life.

9

Light for Each Other

We are each an ember of the mind of God and we are each sent to illumine the other through the dark passages of life to sanctuaries of truth and peace.

Joan Chittister, OSB,
Wisdom Distilled from the Daily

We are light for each other. There are so many ways this happens—some profound and life-changing, others brief and simple yet still illuminating the shadowed steps of the human journey.

In the Easter Vigil liturgy of the Catholic Church, there is a beautiful prayer called the Exsultet that follows the lighting of the Easter candle. During the procession each person in the congregation holds a small, unlit, white candle. The flame from the Easter candle is passed to the candles of those standing nearby; they in turn each pass the flame to others around them, until, one by one, the candles of everyone in the darkened church are set aglow with the flame of the Easter fire.

The choir sings, "Exult all creation . . . Jesus Christ is risen! . . . Darkness vanishes forever."

A line of the prayer describes the "flame divided but undimmed." Even though the one flame from the Easter candle enkindles hundreds of flames throughout the gathering, it is no less bright in its own shining. In much the same way, when we pass on the light within us, the light of our own courage and caring, humor and hope, our own glow does not lessen. On the contrary, sharing our light with another increases the light for us all.

There are many ways that we are light for each other. My examples in the next few chapters are not exhaustive, but each has been important to me.

✸ *We shine light when we check on each other.*

A simple way we illumine life for one another is by calling or dropping by, e-mailing or sending a card: "How are you?" "I'm thinking of you." "Is everything okay?" This is especially meaningful in times of illness or emergency, times of real potential dark.

My grandson Jacob checked on me one day that I will always remember. It was September 11, 2001. He was five years old.

My husband and I live in a ten-story condo building on the water on an island near downtown Tampa. A developer named Davis built the island in the 1920s out of earth that was dredged up when the harbor was deepened for bigger ships to come into the port. The little town where Jacob lives does not have any tall buildings; very few houses even have a second story. He does not understand the concept of apartments, so he thinks the whole condo building belongs to us. He calls it "Grandma's castle" and thinks the bridge to Davis Island is the drawbridge over my moat.

On September 11, when Jacob saw the television pictures of the plane hitting the tall tower, he cried out, "That's where Grandma lives! Oh no! That plane hit Grandma's castle!" Silvia, his mom, tried to assure him that it was not my building, that it was far away, but until he could reach me by phone, he was terrified that I had been lost in the collapse of my castle. He was very relieved to hear my voice.

"Grandma, Grandma, are you okay?"

"Yes, Jacob, I'm okay. That terrible thing happened far, far away. What about you, Jake, are you okay?"

"I'm better now," he said softly. We talked awhile, then hung up.

Later Silvia told me he came to her, asking, "Do you think there were other grandmas in those castles that fell far away?"

She said very sadly, "Yes, Jacob, I'm afraid that there were."

"Where are they now?" he asked.

"They are with God now, loving their grandchildren more than ever," she answered, swallowing the huge lump in her throat.

"Do they know that?" he persisted.

"I don't know, Jacob. Why don't we pray that they do?"

That night, and every night since, Jacob prays for the children who lost their grandmas—or their grandpas, or their moms or dads, or anyone they loved—when the castles fell. It is as if he is asking God to check that they are okay. I know his prayer lets in the light.

✪ *We give each other light through the way we deal with suffering.*

Having a sense of humor in difficulty is a way of sharing light and hope. One of the first experiences I had of this was with my Uncle Bill Morton. He was the uncle we knew better than any of the others. As his health failed, the way he tried to be playful about his physical frailties made a deep impression on me. He had lost feeling in his legs below his knees and had to use a walker. It was made of a kind of bright aluminum, and he named it "Silver," after the Lone Ranger's horse. When he would begin his painful progress across a room, he would look up and grin and say, "Hi ho, Silver, awaaaay!"

Then there is Sister Agnes, a beloved friend of mine who is in her mid-nineties, a Sister of Providence at St. Mary of the Woods. She once wrote:

Dear Pat,

Thank you for your birthday card and letter, your prayers and love. I am in the infirmary and have gone down from 132 pounds to 94. They can't seem to find the cause. I've been in the hospital for tests, but they don't show anything. The chaplain anointed me a couple of weeks ago. I told him that I'm living according to the scripture. Jesus said to the apostles, "Come apart and rest awhile." I'm coming apart all over, and I'm doing nothing but resting.

Sometimes a sense of gratitude in the midst of suffering becomes a source of light. I think of Charles, a former client of my husband's. Charles is a giant of a man, an African-American in his late thirties. He has been a powerful athlete and an amazing entrepreneur in a completely nonmainstream way, creating his own business in which he has helped homeless people in Tampa have a place to sleep and food to eat, and figured out ways for all kinds of people to exchange skills.

Some time ago Thomas had a stroke and is now paralyzed. He is trying to arrange a way to run his business from a wheelchair. In a recent conversation when my husband asked how he was doing, Thomas replied, "It is hard when I can't even get up to open the window to feel the breeze, but still, I feel pretty good."

"You do?" my husband asked, surprised.

"Well, half the time I do. You see, half the time I am sleeping, and when I'm sleeping, I'm dreaming, and when I'm dreaming I'm walking, and I don't even know I'm dreaming and I'm happy. It's hard when I wake up and realize it's a dream, but I tell myself I'll be back tonight walking again. God blesses me with dreams."

People pour light into the world when they are able to be grateful in the midst of suffering. This is also true when someone models graceful acceptance of suffering.

A priest I met at a conference was talking at dinner about a fellow Jesuit, a famous scholar and brilliant theologian whose books have been translated into many languages. He suffered a stroke in his late fifties and now has to be wheeled around. He has trouble completing even one sentence.

"He is the most influential man in our province."

"Because of all his contributions to theology?" I asked.

"Oh, no. Because of his surrender to God after his stroke. He accepted it with such courage. We Jesuits know how to be brilliant. We don't know how to be broken, to simply trust in God. He shows us that every single day."

✪ *A special light is kindled when people respond out of a largeness of heart.*

I am remembering an incident when I was edging out of our condo driveway. Unfortunately, a tall hedge at the side of our gate blocks the view of the sidewalk from the driveway, and the driveway from the sidewalk. I had almost cleared the gate when I felt a great *thump*, and all of a sudden a man was rolling across the hood of my car in front of my windshield! A man on a bicycle had hit the side of my car!

I was absolutely horrified. I had never been in an accident of any kind. I jumped out of the car and ran over to where the man was lying on the pavement. "Are you all right? Are you hurt?"

He got up slowly, looked at his skinned knees, and shook his head. "This is nothing worse than what used to happen to me every day in football practice," he said, and even managed a smile. His graciousness almost dropped me on the pavement!

His bike was badly bent, so we loaded it into my trunk, and I drove him home. I was shaking as I drove, unstrung by a combination of terror and relief. We pulled into his driveway, and he called out to his friend who was working there. We blurted out to her what had happened; she looked at us both, then said to me, "How are *you*? You look worse than he does!"

It is hard to put into words what her compassion meant to me. At that moment when her dearest friend was scraped up, she still had room to care about how I was. Typically in situations like this, there would be blaming, swearing, accusations, and "call my lawyer" statements. These people were gracious instead of blaming, generous instead of abusive. Both of them gave me the light of largeness of heart.

✿ *Light radiates from affirmation.*

Sometimes one affirmation makes a lifelong difference. I witnessed a remarkable example of this not long ago. I was giving a parish mission in Louisville, Kentucky, and I was staying at the motherhouse of the Louisville Ursulines in their guest area for the week.

Sunday afternoon we had quite a bit of excitement. I was working on my talk for that night when I saw several strange bright flashes of light, eruptions very close together. Then the fire alarm went off. Because many of the sisters are elderly, the volume is set so people could hear it whether they have hearing aids or not. On the loud speaker system a voice said, "Sisters, go to the west of the building." I had no idea which direction the building faced, but before long sisters began coming down the corridor to where I was staying, and they assured me this was the west corner.

No one knew what was wrong exactly, but it seemed that something had caused the transformer to blow. Two huge fire trucks arrived, and while firemen were tramping through the building searching for the trouble, a wonderful thing happened.

One of the firemen was a big man about six feet, four inches tall in huge boots and bulky waterproof overalls held up with almost comically colorful suspenders. He stopped in mid-stride and looked at a tiny older sister wearing a modified habit and veil. "Sister Joan Marie, is that you?"

"Why, yes," she replied.

"Do you remember me?" he asked.

She looked up at him, amused and puzzled and affectionate at the same time. "Well now, dear, help me out a little."

"You taught me in the third grade," he said.

"Perhaps if you told me your name, dear," she said. "You've changed a bit since then." (Two feet taller and thirty-five years older!)

"I'm Ron Watson."

"Why, yes, dear, of course!" she said, smiling. "You had two brothers. You were the middle. You used to clean my erasers for me after school."

"I did! Nearly every day. Sister, I loved being in your class. You didn't think I was stupid because I had a hard time reading. And you liked me." He said it with such a tone of wonder, it made my throat ache. She had *liked* him.

"Well of course, dear, how could anyone keep from liking *you*?" she said, beaming at him. "And here you are helping me out again in this emergency," she continued, gently leading him back to the task at hand in the darkened motherhouse.

Thirty-five years later he still remembered being touched by her affirmation. Being in her third grade class had made a difference to him then, and still did now.

✪ *It is a source of light to witness people loving each other.*

I am very touched by love in families, especially by love in marriages where people have been together a long time. So many marriages do not make it, or, even if they do, what is evident is the great strain it takes to stay together. It is heartening to know a couple who seem to love each other more and more deeply.

I think of my mother- and father-in-law who have been married more than sixty years. The past few years have brought a lot of illness, surgeries, and pain for them, first for one and then for the other. They live by themselves in their own home, and they take turns taking care of each other with thoughtfulness, patience, and humor that move me deeply.

Another relationship that glistens for me is a couple I first knew when they were dating. I went to school with her for years and listened to her excitement when she met him. They married quite young and had seven children. After about twenty years, she got cancer. The disease would be in remission for a while and then return. The final time, it moved in quickly, and she died before Christmas.

I was speaking in their city some months later, and I met her husband for breakfast. He seemed very willing to talk about her, telling me openly about her last weeks, her death, her funeral. He then spoke freely about their years together. I asked him if he ever sensed her presence now. He thought for a while, then smiled very poignantly.

"I feel it the most last thing at night. We used to have this bedtime ritual. I would say, 'Good night, sleep tight, don't let the bedbugs bite.' Then she always added the next line, which I had never heard before I married her: 'But if they do, grab your shoe, and whack 'em in two.'"

He was quiet for a moment, then said, "I think it was kind of a metaphor for all the problems we faced together through the years. Now, when I turn out the light, it is as if I can hear her chuckling, adding 'grab your shoe, whack 'em in two.' She's telling me that she's still beside me, helping with it all."

Hearing that from him meant a great deal to me. It seems such a fine image for how we stand with each other in fighting back against the fears and resentments and tiny biting negatives that eat at our peace and infest our gladness. His story captures the playfulness and support, forgiveness and sense of adventure we can give each other, as they did, for so many years.

The next morning I woke up in the hotel still thinking of the wonderful conversation. It was a while before I became aware that I was scratching my leg. I pulled up the hem of my nightgown and looked: a small red bite. Something had bitten me in bed! A bedbug? It was as if I could hear my old friend laugh out loud in her deep, rich, roughened-by-smoking laugh: "Hey, Pat! Don't forget to whack 'em in two!"

✪ *Light can come to us from our loved ones who have died.*

I was thinking of my friend and the bug bite when I read an editorial in *America* magazine by George Anderson, SJ, reflecting on November as the month in which we particularly remember our dead. He included this passage from theologian Karl Rahner:

> The great and sad mistake of many people . . . is to imagine that those whom death has taken, leave us. They do not leave us. They remain! Where are they? In the darkness? Oh, no! It is we who are in darkness. We do not see them, but they see us. Their eyes, radiant with glory, are fixed upon

our eyes. . . . Oh, infinite consolation! Though
invisible to us, our dead are not absent. . . .
They are living near us, transfigured . . . into
light, into power, into love.[1]

✪ *Children, new to this life, can give light.*

I like considering light from those who have
gone to God right before I reflect on the radiance
from those so newly come.

There is so much light from children. Last week
I got eight hugs in a row from Kadee's little Trishy.
Named for me and her other grandmother, also a
Patricia, this tiny two-year-old is utterly hilarious, a
significant power in her own right, even with three
brothers. This particular afternoon she had put
shorts on her head like a hat, the pink legs sticking
up over her blonde curls. She was singing along to
herself when suddenly she ran over and hugged
me. Melting, I hugged her back, then loosened my
grip to let her go. But she tightened her squeeze
again, making small sounds. I was really touched.
She is so much her own self that she does little she
does not want to do. I let her go again, and once
again she hugged me tight. Eight times. It is
interesting how sense memory works. I can replay
that day and feel those hugs as if they were
happening now, shining light on my moment.

Hunter and Hannah, Boo and Caroline's fair,
bright children, gave me a gift of light recently that
I was later able to pass on. I was baby-sitting for
them so their mom and dad could go out to a
special dinner. Halfway through the evening they
started telling me about something they had seen.

They are so good at telling tales together, each filling in what the other leaves out, eyes sparkling, loving the process. They were recalling incidents from a favorite TV program, *America's Funniest Home Videos.* The video was of a family who, on some occasion, had lined up on the patio tallest to smallest. They were doing a kind of dance, each with his or her hands on the shoulder of the one in front of them, in a sort of Conga line. The family dog was watching the line, then went to the end of it, stood on his hind legs, put his paws on the child at the end of the line, and joined in the dance!

Telling the story, Hunter and Hannah began to act it out. "I'll be the dog, I'll be the dog! No, let's get a dog!" They ran to the bedroom and brought back a toy Labrador from their vast stuffed-toy collection. Hunter balanced it on Hannah's shoulders, he got in front, and they started to dance. They sang a little song as they did this—not much tune to it, but it had a definite rhythm: "Da doot du da doot du, da doot doot doot!" Each time they did this, they would dissolve into laughter.

Next, they got the idea of adding other animals. They got a teddy bear to follow the dog, and then a mouse to follow the bear. They then discussed who could come after the mouse, according to size: a gerbil next? And then an ant? Each time they added someone to the line, they would repeat the refrain: "Da doot du da doot du, da doot doot doot!" This was followed by helpless laughter, waves and waves and waves. I laughed until I got the hiccups, which they thought was funnier still. We did this for about an hour. Calming them down to go to sleep was no small feat, but finally we managed to turn in.

A week later I flew to Knoxville where my sister Peggy lives, and then she and I flew to upstate New York where our sister Mary is. There are just the three of us in the family, and we had not been together for five years. In that time, Peggy's "brain thing" had turned the world around, and Mary's mental illness and diabetes had escalated. As we sat together the first evening, we could feel the undertow of gathering dark. Someone asked, "How are the children?" And I thought of Hunter and Hannah and the dance.

I hesitated to tell the story—surely it was in the category of "you had to be there" for it to strike you funny—but it seemed that anything lighthearted was worth trying. I began to describe the scene, and I got tickled all over again at the memory of their little faces. I tried to imitate the refrain. Pretty soon Mary pulled Peggy up. She put her hand on Peggy's shoulder and said, "Come on! Let's do it." So I got up behind her, and away we went around the room: "Da doot du da doot du, da doot doot doot!"

We laughed until we cried, and then we laughed some more. If there had been a dog in Mary's house, surely it would have joined the line. And bears and mice and ants, and who knows who. Angels, maybe. Hunter and Hannah had no idea their story would lead the sisters in a dance. The dance of life. Right when the dark was rising.

10

Meeting in Kindness

"As high as 90 percent of all those who help after emergencies are volunteers. Less than 1 percent are looters or scalpers."

Todd McMullin,
Disaster Help Network Project Manager

In times of darkness, helping others lets in the light.

This dynamic was so vivid after 9/11. People here in Tampa stood in line twelve to fourteen hours to give blood when it still seemed there would be people alive at Ground Zero who would need it.

So many people gave or sent support for the rescue workers. Two stories about food have stayed in my memory, linked by the contrast. The first was of a five-star restaurant in Manhattan. The chef sent the rescue workers dinner night after night:

filet mignon and lobster and lamb chops; every kind of elegant dessert.

The contrasting source of food was from men in prison. Their need to be of help was made more urgent, I imagined, by the realization that their lives were more of a burden to the city than a contribution. The way I heard the tale was that somehow an idea spread among the men, gathering great positive response, that they could give up their food that day to send to the rescue workers. They stood in the cafeteria line, and instead of putting food on a tray for themselves, they packed the food in a box to send to someone working in the rubble of the towers. They felt grateful to go hungry so they had something to give.

There is a beautiful passage in Rachel Remen's book, *My Grandfather's Blessings,* where her rabbi grandfather is passing on to her the ancient Jewish wisdom:

> When we offer our blessings generously, the light in the world is strengthened, around us and in us. The Kabbalah speaks of our collective human task as *Tikkun Olam;* we sustain and restore the world.[1]

My sister Mary recently articulated how the light in her world is strengthened when she is able to help others. She told me it is the main thing that keeps her from despair. She has been seriously mentally ill for more than twenty years. Now her diabetes has reached the point where medications alone are not enough, and she must have injections every day. Her doctor has told her that there is a chance that she will someday go blind.

The worst part, she says, is the sense of endlessness, the permanence, the lack of hope that she will ever possibly be better. This is worse for her than any of her symptoms. She is only fifty-eight, and the weight of possibly decades more of struggle seems always to be lurking in her consciousness. Not long ago, I asked if there were anything at all that helped, anything that broke through the unending sense of condemnation to this fate. "Is there," I asked, "any window that lets in the light?"

When she called back some days later with an answer, I was glad to hear excitement in her voice. "Here's what makes a difference! I've really paid attention since we talked. Here is what distracts me from preoccupation with the endless road of suffering ahead: I get a break from feeling it when I am doing something loving for someone else. Someone who needs my help. But it has to be in person. And they have to want it. They need to respond somehow, so that I can see it matters to them."

She laughed. "Unappreciated efforts do little for my pain! Something has to pass between us, something given and received. Their receiving is as important as the gift. When I make Dino dinner, and his eyes light up. Or share a cigarette with someone who has run out. Or take my blind friend to the store. Or the lady who can't afford a cab to see her doctor. That's what helps. In that time when we're together in the kindness, I guess you'd say, my endless illness disappears. What I'm saying is that it helps me to know I can still be a blessing to someone else."

I had tears in my eyes when I hung up the phone, and I thought of another passage in *My Grandfather's Blessings:*

> The capacity to bless life is in everybody. The power of blessing is not diminished by illness or age. On the contrary, our blessings become even more powerful as we grow older. They have survived the buffeting of our experience. . . .
>
> A blessing is not something that one person gives another. A blessing is a moment of meeting, a certain kind of relationship in which both people involved remember and acknowledge their true nature and worth, and strengthen what is whole in one another. . . . [2]

This seems to me to be exactly what my sister was saying: The *mutuality* of blessing is enormously important in helping each other to live. We are in this *together!*

In the fall of 2004 in central Florida we were battered by four hurricanes in forty-four days. Week after week after week, we were either anxiously watching, or bracing for the actual impact, or dealing with the aftermath. With the power out for days, even weeks, we had great need—literally and figuratively—for letting in the light.

Through the prism of those storms came all the colors of light we have been reflecting on in the chapters of this book, but the most striking radiance of light came from helping each other. The outpouring was astounding. Agencies coordinating efforts reported two hundred calls per hour.

Touching stories filled the pages of newspapers: neighbors helping neighbors; retirees going in vans to ravaged places, hauling tools and wood and shingles, water and food and ice; little girls baking and selling cookies to make money to donate to school programs called "Kids Helping Kids."

Total strangers saw a need and pitched in. One woman in a hard-hit town told a friend of mine this story: She had been in line all morning at the only gas station nearby that had a generator to pump the gasoline. When she got back to her damaged home, she found that someone had covered her ripped-up roof with plastic weighted down with bricks, enough to keep the rain out until more repairs could be made. When she asked the man next door if he had seen who had done this, he said some stranger with a truck came by just looking for anyone who could use a hand.

"I checked him out real close," her neighbor said, "making sure he wasn't looting or some such thing. Here's what he told me: 'Years ago someone did this plastic thing for me when parts of my roof blew off in Hurricane Donna, and it really made a difference. Saved so much more damage to our rooms. I'd just like to pass on that favor.'"

Three of the four hurricanes hit the area in the center of the state where my children and their families live. It was powerful for me to see them responding to the storms, to watch how courageous and creative they were dealing with their own damage, pitching in for family efforts, checking on elderly friends, organizing neighborhood work parties and barbecues of food from freezers without power. Randy volunteered as a nurse and EMT in a

Red Cross shelter. Boo and a boyhood friend went out with food and water and ice in search of immigrant workers who were afraid to come to shelters or food stations for help.

Teams of power company workers came from all over the country. Again and again they reported how important it was to them that what they did mattered so much. One man from a Pennsylvania power company said, "It was worth the heat, the humidity, the mud, the mosquitoes, the snakes, even the gators, to hear the cheers and see the faces of the children on the streets of the neighborhoods when we could connect the power again.

Throughout the long storm season, I was struck by my sister's crucial point in the whole dynamic of helping: It is mutual. It is not just the person who is doing the giving who contributes. The receiving is as important as the giving. What produces the brilliance of the light is that we meet in the kindness. In the exchange we strengthen one another.

As I look back on those days, one experience of mine stands out. It was just before the third hurricane. A very important task was to fill up the car with gas not only because evacuation might be necessary, but also because gas might not be available for days or weeks after the storm passed through.

I had been waiting over an hour in a line that stretched for blocks. Finally, I was second in line. The woman in the car in front of me was swiping her credit card and reaching for the fuel nozzle. Big problem! Her gas tank opening was on the wrong side. There was no way the hose could reach around to the far side of her sleek, black car. In desperation she tried the other two hoses, but they were not even close to being long enough. "No, no," she cried, leaning against the gas pump and pounding on it with her fist.

At first I thought, "How can she not know where the gas tank is?" Then it occurred to me that it probably was not her car. Perhaps her boss had ordered her to take it out to find gas. She started to get back in the car and just drive off.

I jumped out and called to her, "Why don't you just pull up and turn around, come back in on the other side?"

"You mean you would be willing to let me do that?" She was stunned.

"Of course!" I said. "Don't forget. . . ." I waited till she was really looking at me before I continued, "we're in this *together.*"

Tears came down her face. "That is the nicest thing anyone has said to me in a long time."

People in the opposite line moved their cars enough so she could turn around. She filled her tank, then walked over to me and said, "Thank you. I really mean it. Thanks."

It was such a little thing, but it was a blessing exchanged. Her receiving was as significant to me as my giving was to her. This is such an important point because we can feel so worthless when we are not the one giving. The receiving is just as important. We meet in the kindness. Together we can sustain and restore the world.

11

Meeting in Prayer

In the tender compassion of our God, the dawn from on high shall break upon us, to shine on those who dwell in darkness and the shadow of death, and to guide our feet into the way of peace.

"Canticle of Zechariah,"
The Book of Common Prayer (Luke 1:78-79)

Sometimes we cannot do anything physical to help someone, but we can pray. After hurricane Charley, many in Tampa gathered at the Franciscan Center spontaneously and prayed for those injured and homeless and struggling because of the storm. I could feel the loving energy go out of that chapel to the shelters and roofless houses and lines of people waiting for water and food.

Energy is real. Physicists assure us that nothing that exists is static; everything is energy. Prayer is energy. It goes out from us and impacts reality. How this happens, how our prayer somehow interacts with the energy of the Divine, we cannot explain. But prayer makes a difference, as medical studies have shown.

What fascinates me is the mutuality of prayer. It is another example of the mutuality of blessing, of Remen's "moment of meeting." Whether we know it or not, when we meet in the moment of prayer, we strengthen the light in the world.

Years ago I stayed in a section of a large convent in upstate New York, the motherhouse of the Sisters of St. Francis of Allegany. They call the wing where I was staying the Retiro. The sisters who live there direct retreats and meet in their small chapel at special times for prayer. I had come to speak at a conference sponsored by the whole community, but I shared meals and prayer with the sisters in the Retiro. Each night they prayed for various needs and people in our world. The category that caught my attention most was their prayers for people who were traveling, especially people on the road for a living: truckers, delivery services, bus drivers.

I knelt there in that chapel with a vivid picture in my head of a driver of some huge eighteen-wheeler on a highway, the driver drinking coffee to stay awake, rolling down the window to let more air into his cab, trying to sing with the radio, fighting sleep, weaving a little in his lane. And suddenly the drowsiness is gone. His head clears. He sits up straight, alert, realizing that he has been in danger, but that the danger is over. "What happened?" he asks himself in passing, with no idea that a little group of nuns a thousand miles away has been praying for him.

Years later when some of the same Franciscan group had a breakdown on a Florida turnpike, it was a trucker who stopped and helped them. I smiled to myself, delighted, when I heard that story. Little did they know they had met before.

The mutuality of prayer was demonstrated to me very dramatically during my health crisis with the carotid artery buildup.

At this time in my life, I was sometimes awake in the middle of the night. Before this sleeplessness began to be a pattern, I had never prayed for long lists of people on any regular basis. But in these post-midnight interludes, I had begun praying for people in my life. Picturing their faces, imagining them surrounded by God's love, blessing them. I sometimes imagined that I put my hand on their heads or made the sign of the cross on their foreheads.

One by one, I would pray for my family, friends, and colleagues, people who mattered to me, people whose lives had intersected with mine. Most were people I knew well, but others were people, who, for some reason, had just stayed in my memory even though I seldom saw them. A few were people I had never really met but felt drawn somehow to pray for.

There was a geography to it. I would picture where they lived, and work my way south to north, east to west, and back again. Some nights I could hardly make it past my youngest grandchild before

I fell back to sleep. Other times I got through the list and would start again.

Then my doctor ordered a test called an MRA to image the blockage in my arteries. Similiar to an MRI, this particular kind of test is done in a narrow closed tube, which, if one is claustrophobic at all, can be an ordeal. Besides being worried about the claustrophobia, I was concerned because I had a bad cough, the kind that causes a constant tickle in the back of the throat, producing almost continuous dry coughing. I knew I had to hold perfectly still for this test. I called the technician the day before my appointment to ask if coughing could be a problem.

She laughed. "A problem? Honey, you can't even swallow, much less cough. A cough produces the same image on the screen as a total blockage. We have to toss the whole test if there is a cough."

Whew! No coughing at all. And swallowing was even out, which meant no cough drops. The test could be as long as thirty minutes, and I had hardly gone even three minutes without a cough in days. Just thinking of not coughing made me want to cough all the more.

My heart sank. Then she said, "Let's just try it. Don't get uptight. We'll give it a try, and if it doesn't work, we'll just do it another day when you are better."

So I agreed. The night before, I was once again awake for hours in the middle of the night. I did my usual wide-awake thing of praying for my dear ones, and in the middle of that I thought, "This is what I'll do in the tube tomorrow! Praying takes my mind off my night worries. Maybe praying for them will help me not to cough, not to panic."

The next day when I had been in the tube for less than five seconds, I broke into a sweat. Immediately, I felt a terrible urge to cough. "Pray," I told myself, "pray." I began with my daughter, picturing her vividly, trying to take my mind off my strain and just be with her in the surrounding love of God.

Then something happened that was totally unexpected. I will never be able to explain it. Instead of my blessing her, as my little imaginary ritual goes, she stepped forward and blessed me. Made the sign of the cross on my forehead, smiled, and stepped back. Her husband stepped up next and did the same thing. Then their children, one by one. Then Randy came. Then Silvia. Their boys. One by one. Then Boo. Then Caroline. Then their son and daughter. One after another, each of the people from my awake-in-the-dark list came to me and blessed *me.* I was fascinated to see who stepped up next. Some people came more than once. The last one was my husband, grinning. Just as he stepped up, I heard the technician say, "That's it, you're done. You never coughed. You didn't even swallow! It looks great!"

As she eased me out of the tube, she looked at me in astonishment.

"What is it?" I asked.

She said, "You're ... well ... it's almost like you're glowing. Your face is full of light."

"Do you think it was the stuff you put in my veins?" I asked.

"No, honey. No, I don't. I've never seen this before. I guess you're just relieved you're finally out of there."

What I am, I said to myself, is filled with blessing.

When we pray for people, it makes a difference. It makes a difference to them, and it makes a difference to us.

"The dawn from on high shall break upon . . . those who dwell in darkness."

There is an exchange of grace.

12

Light for Prayer[1]

The Kabbalah teaches that the Holy may speak to you from its many hidden places at any time. The world may whisper in your ear, or the spark of God in you may whisper in your heart.

Rachel Naomi Remen, M.D.,
My Grandfather's Blessings

The spark of God can whisper to us anywhere. I heard that whisper comically at a 9:00 a.m. Mass where a father and a little boy, about three or four years old, were sitting in front of me in the third row. The homily was very long, and dad had used up all the Cheerios, had gone through all the books, had gotten out all the crayons for scribbling on the parish bulletin. Finally, the boy said in a very loud voice, "Is he *ever* going to sit down?"

Well, that did it, there was nothing for the father to do but take him out. So he picked up the boy and headed down the center aisle. Everyone in the church, including the priest giving the homily, was watching them go. The boy was looking over his father's shoulder, and suddenly he realized that he was the total center of attention. This was not an opportunity to waste! Putting his arms out toward us in a pleading gesture, he called, "Pray for me, pray for me."

"Pray for us all," said the priest, "in the name of the Father, the Son, and the Holy Spirit. Amen." And sat down.

God whispers in our hearts when we pray for one another—and when we help each other pray. Through the years I have been significantly helped to pray by five pieces of advice that have brought more light into my prayer.

The first piece of advice was given to me many years ago. I was in a stage with prayer where I was trying hard to follow strict traditional lines. I was finding this effort, if I could have admitted it, quite burdensome. A very wise friend said to me, "Pat, you are not a monk. Stop trying to pray the way monks do. Look for a way to pray that really appeals to you, that you can look forward to. Stop praying in a way that puts that serious 'I-*will*-be-disciplined' look on your face! Why would God want to hang out with you in that mood?" This affectionate challenge shone light into my prayer.

The second piece of advice came in an article by a Jesuit named Patrick Carroll. I read it about twenty-five years ago, and I have never forgotten his main point. It reminded me of something

Teresa of Avila once said, that we do not go to prayer to talk much, but to love much.

Carroll's point was a little different. He wrote that many of us attempt to spend more and more time in prayer trying to show our great love for God. But, he argued, the real purpose of going to prayer is to let God love *us,* to deepen our sense and conviction of God's powerful love for us.

Somehow that advice refocused the energy of my prayer. The definition of prayer in the *Baltimore Catechism,* long engraved on my spiritual life, was "raising the mind and heart to God." For years I went to prayer feeling that it was up to me to do the raising; that the effort, the energy began with me.

Carroll's article reversed this for me. As I came to prayer, I simply tried to be aware that the energy began with God, that the energy is all Love. With that shifted focus, praying became lighter once again.

The third piece of advice was additionally freeing. Not long ago I came across a little book called *The God Who Won't Let Go* by a Dutch Jesuit named Peter van Breemen. He wrote:

> When prayer seems lacking in fruitfulness, usually the reason is that we have tried to do too much. Years of experience have convinced me of this. 'Doing too much' might mean that we are straining, unwittingly trying to force an experience of God. This only makes us tense, and that tension can block the gentle movement of God....Resist the inclination to make prayer productive. [2]

I laughed out loud when I read that.

The best of my prayer these days shows the effect of these three strands of wisdom. I pray at times and in settings that really appeal to me, that I look forward to. My favorite way to pray is having coffee with God early in the morning, looking out at the water of Tampa Bay. Every day the sky and wind and water are a canvas communicating God's love. The interplay of light is infinitely lovely. Birds and fish are on the move: dolphins and mullet, osprey and pelicans, herons, gulls, and cormorants. I watch and listen, in wordless gratitude, sipping coffee and letting in love. When I am not home, I try to find a window for my prayer time so I can look out at the trees or the sky. Or I close my eyes and return to a setting in my memory.

After the coffee, sometimes I read the scripture of the day or a little of another book. Sometimes I meditate with a mantra. On different days I am drawn to different ways. The key for me is not to strain, to follow what is appealing, to pay attention to what communicates God's loving presence.

Next to early morning prayer, I love to pray at sunset. I cannot wait to see what God will come up with for color and pattern in clouds and clearings. One evening there was a thick haze, the sunset simply a sky of long, gentle, slow-fading rose. Watching it was a prayer of quiet companioning, as in an old and easy friendship.

The best rhythm for me is early and late, the beginning of the day and the end. Praying at those times gives a kind of prayer awareness to my day, an ongoing *being-with*, a sense of presence that I return to when I can.

I am able to do this more some days than others. Some days I seem to hit the ground running and have little awareness of anything other than a series of urgent tasks or concerns. I chafe at slowing down. Here is where the fourth piece of advice helps me. It came from my friend Loni: "When you can't slow yourself down enough to pray, use the times when you are *forced* to slow down. Think of them as God carving out places to meet."

Since then I have tried to see forced stops in the flow of the day as invitations to return to the awareness of God's presence. It is as if God uses various opportunities to try to wave me down: when I am at a long red light, stuck on the freeway, in a checkout line that does not move, put on endless hold on the phone, or waiting through a drawn-out delay for something to come up on my computer screen. When I recognize the opportunity (which is not always!), I try to slow down my breathing and let the awareness of God's presence return. This lightens the pressures of my day.

Another time of prayer that never used to be part of my life is the wide-awake, middle of the night, clear-sign-of-getting-older time frame. This was not in my rhythm in younger years. Unless a child or a phone call in the dark woke me, I would sleep straight through. I am no longer the champion solid sleeper I once was. This is a new era!

For quite a while, I dreaded this sleeplessness. All the things I worry about would come out and pounce on me: our world with its war and hatred and endless retaliation; the lives of people I love, with their suffering and sadness; problems of my own. The darkness would weigh me down, and I would turn and toss indefinitely.

I began to use prayer to deal with the thoughts and images that kept me tossing. I would begin by opening my awareness of God's loving presence. Then I would pray for situations and people one by one, trying to imagine God's loving energy flowing into the place or the people, grounding and surrounding them, holding and enfolding them.

Doing this one night, I remembered my mother's favorite prayer—the fifth source of helpful advice.

I could laugh out loud picturing Mom's face at the very idea of being quoted on this topic. My mother was a person of very strong faith, but she was not one for "making a big deal about it." "I am not holy-go-pious," she would say, as if she had been delivered from some intolerable burden. She was entirely matter-of-fact about God. I can just see her rolling her eyes at the thought of being included as a source of advice about prayer.

In the last Holy Week of her life, I was staying with her in her little apartment. She was far too sick to go to church, and when I returned from the Good Friday service, I was explaining to her how the parish had offered a "Seven Last Words" service. Members of the parish had been asked to give reflections on what the various gospels record as the last words of Jesus. I told her that my sister Peggy had given the meditation on Jesus' saying, "Into your hands I commend my spirit" (Lk 23:46).

"Oh, I think that is the most important one," Mom said. "That is what it is all about, all our lives long: putting ourselves in God's hands. I hope I am lucid enough at the end to remember to say that when I am dying. I'd really like to say that when I die."

She looked down, uneasy with this conversation so unlike her usual style. After a pause, she continued: "If I am not conscious, or if I am somehow too distracted, I hope one of you girls will say it for me: 'Into your hands I commend my spirit.'"

The afternoon of Mom's death, my sister Peggy was there. Mom was not conscious at the end, and Peggy remembered. Holding Mom's hands in hers, she said the words for her: "Into your hands I commend my spirit."

This has become the prayer that I hold onto for the many concerns that are in my heart, especially in the middle of the night. Into God's hands I commend my loved ones, my fears and dreams, our struggling nation, our world so torn with terror and revenge and countless kinds of pain. I can feel myself lighten in this praying. Into God's hands— those hands that alone can hold and heal, bring life from death, be Light that the darkness will never overcome—I commend it all.

13

Photosynthesis of Trust

Knowing how to receive and remember goodness is, in fact, the best way to prepare for trusting when goodness seems absent.

Demetrius Dumm, OSB,
Cherish Christ Above All

Commending ourselves and all we care for into God's hands requires trust. There is no greater source of light than the gift of trusting God. It is the primal grace at the very heart of spiritual life.

I am grateful to Fr. Demetrius Dumm for his powerful clarity on this truth in scripture. In his speaking and writing, he keeps emphasizing the central role of trust.

Dumm says we never grow up spiritually until we learn that we are radically dependent on God. Sooner or later, we have to face the fact that we are not in control. Life, no matter what path we choose, leads to challenges we never imagined. The

realization that we can never meet the challenges
through our power alone forces us to address our
dependence on God. If we do not trust God,
realizing our radical dependency can seem like
deliverance into danger rather than a homecoming.

Dumm points out that we cannot just make up
our minds to trust. It is not something we can
simply *will* ourselves to do. Trust comes only when
we experience ourselves as deeply loved. This is
the key step in our spiritual development, just as it
is the key step in the psychological development of
the human person.

According to psychologist Eric Erikson, learning
to trust is the first stage of human development. A
child learns to trust because he or she has
experiences of being loved, of being concretely
cared about: fed, held, clothed, kept safe, treated
with affection.

In exactly the same way, in order to trust God,
we have to know we are loved by God.

> We must not underestimate the difficulty of
> trusting . . . we must reflect constantly upon
> those signs of God's love . . . which make our
> trusting possible. . . . This remembrance must
> be of a goodness experienced, and not just
> heard or read about.[1]

We must *know* we are loved—not in the abstract,
not because someone tells us, but because we have
concrete experiences of goodness that communicate
that we are deeply, personally loved, just as we are.

This perspective from Dumm has been
immensely reassuring to me. I have sometimes felt

that I should just be able to make up my mind to trust, to rally an act of my will, and that it was a failure on my part if I were afraid or overwhelmed. I now am convinced that I cannot do this on my own. I must be aware of God's love for me expressed in experiences of goodness. Focusing on God's goodness is what gives strength to trust. We need to notice the goodness, really let it in, *receive* it, Dumm says, and *remember* it. We need to let in the light.

I am struck by the similarity between this spiritual process and the process of photosynthesis.

Cosmologist Brian Swimme describes the mutation event of photosynthesis that took place 3.5 billion years ago. Photosynthesis enabled life forms to capture sunlight, a process essential for the survival of life on our planet. Without photosynthesis, life would have soon died out. In an amazing feat of biological development, life forms fashioned a molecular net that transformed the shape of the light and held it until energy was needed. The conversion of light into chemical energy became the foundation for the whole food chain of the planet.[2]

Photosynthesis at the heart of the survival of physical life offers a metaphor for the survival of our spiritual life. Opening ourselves to goodness begins the process of photosynthesis for our souls. When we receive and remember goodness, somehow the light of the goodness becomes transformed into trust for God, stored in our souls to be called on in times "when goodness seems absent." Drawing on that trust keeps our hope alive in the inevitable times of struggle and darkness.

We have been reflecting on many kinds of goodness in this book, a rainbow of colors in the light of our lives: prayer, laughter, and blessing given and received; affirmation and the witness of courage; places, stories, and refrains for our hearts, like Sharon's gentle "It'll be all raaht." Light pours out around us, but we need to let it in. For the photosynthesis of trust to happen, we have to receive the goodness. Two practical ways of focusing on goodness have made a difference for me.

The first way is the simple act of listing our blessings: naming in some very concrete form, one after another, the goodness in our lives, the things we have to be grateful for. This is an ancient practice, almost a cliché, but I find it very profound.

I was speaking in a parish in St. Louis last spring, and Sarah, the woman who is the lay pastoral associate, came up to the microphone and gave what I thought was a delightful example. The first engaging thing about her story was that the event she described had been initiated by her son, a second-grader named Bryan. One evening in November he said he wanted to do a family art project.

She told us that she had had a very long, hard day when he suggested this, and all she wanted to do was melt into the couch. The last thing she wanted was some project that would make more mess. Only with his insistent pleading and his conning Adam and Sami, his younger brother and sister, into helping him pester her, did she agree to it.

His idea was that they would make a turkey out of construction paper, and then make feathers for its tail, and on each feather they would write something they were grateful for. They would glue or staple or tape the feathers on, one by one, as they thought of something. Each person would read their next feather aloud so they would not duplicate.

They got out all the materials, and she admitted she was still dragging her feet, thinking, "If we can just get this over with I can go to sleep." It had been the hardest year she could remember, the year of the divorce, the year of terrible financial insecurity, a year of much illness. She was feeling more scared than grateful. But as they cut out the different colored feathers after they had made the head and body and feet, she got caught up in the energy of it all.

They had thought they would have one row of feathers and that would be adequate. But one row led to another. And that reminded them of other things they were grateful for. And that reminded them of others. And so it went.

At this point in her story, from a big shopping bag she had carried up with her to the microphone, she pulled out the bird they had made that night and kept on their mantelpiece ever since. There must have been ten rows of feathers. It did not look like a turkey at all. What it looked like was a peacock, the most beautiful of all birds!

"There is a saying, 'Proud as a peacock,' " she said. "They are thought to be vain. But not this peacock! There is no vanity in gratitude. We knew the feathers didn't come from us. They were God's gifts, all of them."

"We could have gone on all night," she said. "At nearly midnight, I realized we'd better go to sleep. That night I slept more deeply than I had in a long, long time."

When we list what we are grateful for, when we take the time and thought to realize how endless the list is, we deepen our trust. We may not have the energy for an art project; we might simply list goodness in quiet by ourselves.

When there is something particularly troubling going on, my friend Mary Kay makes a list of blessings. First, she names and reverences the fear or the pain or the loss. This is an important piece because it is crucial not to discount or belittle our pain. Then she lists the gifts in her life. She tells me that this always helps her perspective, gives her a better sense of balance. It makes trust more possible.

There is another way to open ourselves to goodness that I really enjoy, one I have written about before.[3] It is a simple practice I call "The One Good Thing." It involves having an agreement with friends or family that, on some regular basis, when you get together or get in touch, you will tell each other one good thing that has happened since the last time you talked.

What I have noticed about this practice is that it trains my eye. Because I know that I'll be called upon to name One Good Thing, I am on the lookout for goodness. We see what we are looking for. If we are looking for what goes wrong, we can certainly find it. If we are looking for examples of goodness, there is so much good to discover. This may sound like a little thing, but it can make a big difference.

When my turn for sharing my One Good Thing came in a gathering of friends, I told about a clipping I had received in the mail. It was a guest column that my son Randy had written for their local newspaper, addressed to men and women in the military returning from duty in Iraq.

Randy had been in the Gulf War, and he spoke to them about what they might be experiencing: nightmares, auditory and visual hallucinations, hyper-vigilance, sleep apnea, sheet-soaking night sweats, breaking into tears passing a dead animal on the road. He wrote:

> Don't kill yourself, or even think about it. Remember you made it through that, you can make it through this. Look for the good. It is there. Remember praying for one more day of life? Well, you got it! So enjoy it. . . . Let in the good, be good to those around you. Make a peace treaty with your heart and soul. Welcome home.[4]

Looking for goodness can help us deal with nightmares of many kinds. I see this with my sister Peggy as she is trying to come to terms with "the brain thing," trying to find her way in the painful geography of limitations. ("I can only do about two things right out of four," she said to me one day.)

She is absolutely heroic in how she looks for goodness. She listens with real joy to the wind chimes on her porch whenever there is a breeze. She notices how nice people look in certain colors and tells them so in the grocery store. She savors tea from her dark blue pot—each cup as if it were altogether special. She is amazing on her neighborhood walks: she waves to cars that pass her and smiles; she carries a plastic bag to pick up any trash she finds; she stops and tells people working in their yards how lovely their flowers are or how much she likes the color they painted their door.

"There is so much beauty," she said to me the last time I joined her on a walk. "It feeds me. It keeps me going. It's like God's presence."

I was reminded of an image from Rachel Remen's *My Grandfather's Blessings*. Her rabbi grandfather explained to her that "at some point in the beginning of things, the Holy was broken up into countless sparks, which were scattered throughout the universe. There is a god spark in everyone and everything, a sort of diaspora of goodness."[5] Peggy sees the God spark. She lets it warm her and renew her trust.

It is important not only to see goodness, to receive it, to really let it in as it happens, but also to *remember* it. To keep it alive. To hold on to the light of memories of goodness in the past. One of those memories for Peggy is of goodness at the time of her retirement.

When Peggy's "brain thing" reached the point where her doctor told her she needed to retire, she faced a terrible loss. She was a leader at the Office on Aging, an organization that makes a great difference in the lives of older people in their city and county. Her work gave her great joy, and the daily contact with people in the office community was very life-giving to her. She had worked with some of them for decades.

Resigning also meant giving up her monthly spot on the local "Live at Five" television news program. For about twenty years she had been giving information of special interest to senior citizens. Someone always recognized her at the grocery or in a restaurant. "You're that TV lady," they would say, when they realized why she looked familiar. "I always like it when you come on."

Peggy met with the producer of the show and asked if she could come on one more time to say good-bye, to tell people why she was not going to be on any more, to let them know about her brain condition, and to introduce the woman who would be doing the show in the future. The producer agreed, and Peggy went that Monday to the studio.

When her turn came, she went up on the set and said what she had planned to say. What she did not know was that the station had worked all week making clips of interviews with key people in the aging field in Knoxville, each giving a tribute to Peggy. They aired those clips on the telecast (as she watched), and then the entire crew of the show came on to thank her and tell her how much they would miss her, how much she had come to mean to them over the years. They had a huge sign: "Peggy, you're the best!"

They gave her flowers in an arrangement that was taller than she was! When she got home, she filled every vase she owned with them and put them all over the house.

The next day there was a reception for her after the monthly Council on Aging meeting, a meeting of all the people in the county who work in any related field for seniors. An invitation had gone out to the public.

It seemed to Peggy that everyone she ever knew in Knoxville was there—almost standing-room-only in a huge auditorium. Her daughters and her husband were in the front row. There were spoken tributes of all kinds and a great scrapbook filled with pages of special messages. The mayor declared it Peggy Wirtz Day in Knoxville.

As she told me the story, her voice was soft with wonder, nearly overcome with goodness. It was terribly hard giving up her job. *Terribly* hard. Nothing could take that away. And yet the memory of the outpouring of love and appreciation in what she calls her "sendoff" connects her with what trust in God is all about.

When the light of goodness photosynthesizes into trust, it is not a trust that there will be no pain, no loss, no hardship. It is not a trust that, because God loves us, somehow we will be protected from all harm. It is a trust that we are not alone. It is a trust in the ultimate goodness: whatever happens on the journey, we are held in the hands of Love.

14

Offer It Up

When we live in a world that is full of the
kind of darkness we have now, there's only
one hope and that is to go into it and
through it, and in our small way, never try to
evade our own little bit of darkness but
suffer it consciously.

Helen Luke,
The Way of Woman

When there is great darkness in our lives, we
reach within for trust. Even as we trust, however,
we cannot help but question why the hard things
happen. What does all this mean? Is there any
value to our suffering? I have had many
conversations on these questions in the last few
years with Peggy as she has tried to make sense of
her increasing struggles.

She said, "When we were growing up, people who taught us in our Catholic upbringing would say to us, 'Offer it up.' I'm certainly willing to do that, but then I feel bewildered. What is God going to do with it? Does God have some kind of closet of hard things people offer up? Why would God want it?"

I think this is a very important question: What does God do with suffering?

The term "offer it up" can conjure up images of a primitive deity relishing bloody sacrifices in its honor, or demanding some kind of torturous initiation rite into its sect of chosen followers, or some kind of "eye for an eye" atonement for offenses.

But there is a way in which "offering it up" conveys a profound meaning, at least for me, when it connects us with the suffering of others; when it helps us sustain each other's courage and meet each other in hope.

At the heart of life, I am convinced, there is a place of human oneness, the site of our most profound joys and sufferings, the place our souls take breath.

Some of my favorite books are the old-fashioned English novels of Elizabeth Goudge. The characters, settings, and stories stir something deep within me. Many of them are about the Eliot family. For more than thirty years, an image from the reflections of Hilary Eliot, the country parson, has stayed with me. Hilary is a big, homely man of enormous kindness who limps badly from being wounded in terrible fighting in the war. In Goudge's book *The Heart of the Family,* Hilary is reflecting on suffering

in our lives, how each of us has something to bear.
What Helen Luke in her book *The Way of Woman*
calls our "bit of darkness," Hilary calls the "Thing":

> For there is always the Thing, you know,
> the hidden Thing, some fear or pain or
> shame ... that you can never explain to
> another ... If you just endure it simply
> because you must, like a boil on the neck,
> or fret yourself to pieces trying to get rid of
> it, then it can break you. But if you accept it
> as a secret burden borne secretly for the
> love of Christ, it can become your hidden
> treasure. For it is your point of contact with
> Him ...[and] with every other suffering man
> and woman....
>
> If pain is offered to God as prayer, then pain
> and prayer are synonymous. A sort of
> substitution takes place that is like the old
> Beauty and the Beast. ... The utterly
> abominable Thing that prevents your
> prayer becomes your prayer ...becomes the
> channel of grace for others ... the same with
> the worries and frustrations and irritations
> among which we perpetually live . . . and
> it's the same with joy as with disaster and
> Things; lifted up with that same hard effort,
> earthly joys are points of contact and have
> the freshness of eternity in them. ... Peace
> comes after that effort. Sometimes you're
> conscious of it and sometimes you're not.
> More often not. But it's there just the same
> and is the peace in which God makes your
> soul.[1]

In Hilary's framework, offering up would mean somehow meeting at the point of contact with God and all who rejoice and struggle at the heart of life. This meeting makes a difference. It is the collective human task referred to in the Jewish Kabbalah as *Tikkun Olam,* through which "we sustain and restore the world."

The Christian way of saying it would be that we have a part in redemption. In the Christian tradition, the term redemption essentially refers to the saving action of God through Christ, the reconciliation that brings humanity a new covenant of love with God and one another (2 Cor 5:18-20; Heb 9:15).

There are many metaphors for the process of redemption, metaphors formulated from the theological and cultural understandings of the era in which they were written.

I have been fascinated by a new understanding I first heard when I made a Holy Week retreat at the Franciscan Center in Tampa. The retreat director was theologian and Notre Dame Sister Barbara Fiand. She was explaining redemption from the perspective of quantum physics and cosmology.

It seems there is an archetypal death/resurrection process at the heart of all creation, all the way from subatomic to macrocosmic reality. Fiand quoted quantum theologian Diarmuid O'Murchu as saying, "Calvary precedes resurrection, darkness gives way to light on all these levels."

On the subatomic level every particle of reality has an antiparticle, an opposite that is its exact antithesis. When an electron meets a positron (which is its antiparticle), both of them disappear in an event of mutual destruction, and in their place appear two photons or light particles that instantly depart at the speed of light.[2]

It has now been discovered, Fiand continued, that the same dynamic that happens on the subatomic level occurs at the macrocosmic level, with black holes in space.

A black hole is a collapsed star that was once three times bigger than our sun, now perhaps only a few miles in diameter, an unimaginably dense, burned out, rotating mass. Because of its density, it has a gravitational field strong enough to pull into it everything in its vicinity. The black hole is invisible but can be detected by the activity of stars nearby. They are strangely in motion, orbiting until they are suddenly and completely absorbed into the hole.

For a long time it was assumed that these absorbed stars just vanished forever, but now it has been discovered that, after a time, they are released elsewhere, transformed into a quasi-stellar radio source or quasar. Quasars emit more energy than an entire galaxy of over 150 billion stars.

After explaining the physical process found at all levels of creation, Fiand then connected this process with redemption. In Jesus, the love of God was poured out into human form, and that Love, in total freedom, offered itself on Calvary as the anti-particle to hate, violence, retaliation, ruthlessness. Terrible forces unleashed by sin were faced down on the cross, the sign of contradiction, by the utterly opposite power of totally unselfish love.

122 LET IN THE LIGHT

Destruction followed; there was an earthquake. Even the veil of the temple was torn from top to bottom.

> From noon onward, darkness came over the whole land until three in the afternoon. . . . But Jesus cried out again in a loud voice, and gave up his spirit. And behold, the veil of the sanctuary was torn in two from top to bottom. The earth quaked, rocks were split, tombs were opened . . ." (Mt 27:45, 50-52).

Then . . . transformation . . . Easter! Like a quasar with the light of billions of stars, Love burst the bonds of death in new life.[3]

Our part in the redemptive process can be described in this same framework, going back to Peggy's question: "What does God do with the suffering we offer up?"

God brings us to the point of contact that Hilary Eliot described, the place of meeting with Christ and all other struggling women and men. In that place we are part of redemption itself.

This explanation is consistent with Pope John Paul II's encyclical *Salvifici Doloris, On the Christian Meaning of Human Suffering.*[4] He wrote that there is a certain communion and solidarity of all who suffer. In the mystery of the Body of Christ, a suffering person in any part of the world and in any time in history shares in the work of redemption; we serve the salvation of our brothers and sisters. Our suffering is one with the suffering of Christ.

I find this an extremely powerful concept. Not only are our struggles, our "Thing," not something to be ashamed of, but they can be a source of life.

Offered up in love, they can be the antiparticle to hate. Pope John Paul II's own suffering was a luminous example of this very dynamic. After his death, the outpouring from all over the world could only be described as love.

As we so often hear in the gospels, what is weakest can be a source of strength, what is poor can be a treasure. Again and again, Jesus identified with the poor, "the little ones," the *anawim,* those on the margin. The place he seemed to be most at home, the town of Bethany where Mary and Martha and Lazarus lived, was literally on the margin.

Years ago in a lecture at Notre Dame, I heard scripture scholar Fr. Carroll Stuhlmueller, explain that *beth* in Hebrew means "home" and *ani* is the singular of *anawim.* Literally, Bethany was home for a little one, someone on the margin. When Bethany is mentioned in scripture, the phrase "the town where Simon the leper lived" often follows. Simon lived there because Bethany was on the border, and a leper was not allowed to live any closer to Jerusalem. It was on the margin with the outcasts that Jesus was at home.

The things we struggle with, the sufferings and anxieties, failings and frustrations, all the cripplings of body or mind or spirit, our "Things," bring us to Bethany. And from this place, instead of being outcast, we can be agents of redemption.

When we "offer it up," we gather our suffering in sacrificial love. The root meaning of the word sacrifice is "to make something holy," as in its Latin origin of *sacrum* (holy) and *facere* (to make).[5]

For Peggy, this has emerged as a different way of

being there for older people. At this time in her life, she would be serving by connecting with older people in the Thing, making the struggle holy. The cross of aging. The losses and frustrations, physical conditions and diminished capabilities. Looking for the car keys and the glasses. Mixed up about what day it is. Being baffled by the new telephones that need to be programmed. Afraid of escalators or getting in and out of bathtubs.

Her greatest anguish has been her sense that she does not have anything to offer any more, has no way to help people. Instead of having nothing to offer any more, that very offering becomes the meeting place.

"What does God do with the suffering we offer up?" Peggy had asked me. I have been thinking of that question ever since. I believe that God transforms it into the light of Love, the love that repairs and redeems the world.

15

What If We Can't?

How can we sing the song of the Lord in a
foreign land?

Psalm 137:4 NLT

What if we can't offer it up? What if redemption
seems like a word in a foreign language? What if no
trace of light finds a way into our darkness?

In my treasured collections of funny things that
happened in church is the memory of a father at
Mass with his little boy about four years old. The
boy was very restless, either kicking the pew in
front of him or trying to crawl under and escape.
He kept insisting that he just *had* to go to the
bathroom again.

Finally his dad said, "Timmy, be very still now.
This is the most important part of the Mass. The
priest is going to change the bread and wine into
Jesus." The boy was totally quiet, watching. In the
silence that followed the Consecration, his worried

voice rang out in the church saying, "Dad! It didn't work!"

Sometimes the Consecration does not seem to work.

One of those times came a few days after the birth of my seventh grandchild in seven years, the sixth boy, born on the anniversary of my mother's death.

When I heard that the baby was born, I left the minute I could and after the hundred-mile drive I was moved to tears to see him: beautiful, red-headed Andrew, 9 lbs. 11 oz., healthy and strong-voiced. Silvia was holding him, and Randy and Jacob and George were looking on. Jacob was five and George was three. Everyone was excited and smiling. George said, "Is it really true that we can take him home and keep him a really, really long time?"

Well, anyone who has ever brought a new baby home will understand that the story did not end there. Soon, the idea of keeping the baby a really, really long time stopped seeming like a good idea to George. He and Jacob had not counted on the fact that their mom would have to spend so much time with the baby. They began to have very mixed feelings about this little brother. One day Jacob said, "Mom, you know the dinosaurs?"

"Yes, Jacob," she replied, puzzled.

"Well, do you think babies could be extinct?"

Silvia tried to laugh, but she had a blinding headache from the spinal anesthesia that only seemed to get worse. She could not lie down because, if she did, when she got up she would nearly black out with the returning force of the headache. Because she was so tense with the pain, her milk did not come in for several days. At nearly ten pounds, Andrew was very hungry, and she was experiencing the toe-curling pain of early breastfeeding.

Then, three days after they were home, she discovered that George had head lice! It seems they were passed around at a birthday party. She went into frantic action treating his head, washing every household item not nailed down, stripping all furniture, vacuuming every surface, hour after hour long into the night. She buzzed off his hair, and then Jacob's, and desperately, finally Randy's. Three bald heads. Randy then went through her long dark hair, strand by strand for hours, finding nothing, thank God.

Three days later, the lice terror having passed, George dropped a ball in the toilet. Silvia had no idea it was there, and when she flushed the toilet, it backed up, pouring sewage through the house. It took hours to clean up. Randy had to take the toilet apart to remove the blue-striped ball.

Head lice and sewage, the very opposite of good news.

I got there in time to help with some of it.

Silvia was still trying valiantly to smile. She said, "I know we should praise God in every circumstance. But if I have one more 'circumstance,' I will be praising God in an institution."

And then she started to cry. "Why is God allowing these things to keep happening to me? I haven't slept in five nights. I'm so afraid the baby's losing weight because I have so little milk. My headache is blinding me. I'm terrified the head lice will come back. What if the children get sick from the sewage? We have scrubbed and scrubbed, but did we get it all? I feel like such a bad mother. I feel guilty for saying this, but God seems so far away. So far away. So far away. I know I should trust, but I just feel lost. I'm so ashamed of feeling like this."

I put my arms around her, and she cried and cried.

I cried, too, but I was weeping at her goodness. This precious young woman. Greater love than this, no one has, than to lay down her life for her loved ones. She was laying down her life—her body, her heart, and at this moment it must have seemed to her, her mind—for her family. For this new baby. For all of them. And ashamed because God seemed far away in this avalanche of chaos. Trying to trust, but unable to feel it, she piled guilt and shame onto her burdens.

The next Sunday I visited my friend Benni's church, the First United Methodist Church in Sebring, Florida, and heard one of the finest sermons I can ever remember addressing this issue. The minister, the Reverend Brette Sanford, was preaching on Psalm 137. He read: "Beside the rivers of Babylon we sat and wept at the memory of Zion, hanging our harps on the willow trees. ...How could we sing the song of the Lord in a foreign land?" (1, 2, 4).

He then said:

> Some of us in this church community and
> in our human family have hung up our

harps. Our lives feel as if they were in a foreign land. We are exiled in pain or depression or loss or terrible fear. We cannot sing the song of the Lord. The worst part is that, on top of all the rest, we feel ashamed that we cannot sing.

Do not be ashamed . . . God is weeping with you.

Those of us who are not in exile at this time take up our harps and sing for you. When you can, you will take your harp from the willow again.

We sing for each other the song of the Lord when we can. That's what it means to be church, what it means to be in the human family.

Tears came to my eyes sitting in that church and well up even now. I am so moved by the truth of this. We are in it together, the human journey. Those of us who can are singing for those who, just now, cannot. Holding each other in what belief we have in the good news. Holding each other in our love and God's love, which are one.

It is a source of real strength for me to realize that it is not all up to me. I think so much of my life has been spent being ultraresponsible that it is easy for me to feel as if everything were up to me. It is very consoling to think that others are playing their harps for me when I cannot.

There is a similar image in the book of Exodus that Silvia pointed out to me. During the battle with the Amalekites, Moses had to keep his arms raised.

Whenever his arms fell, the Israelites began to be overcome. As Moses' arms grew heavy, Aaron and Hur supported his arms for him, one on one side, one on the other; and his arms remained firm until sunset when the battle was won (Ex 17:10-14). When Silvia's sister was going through a time of terrible fear for her sick daughter, Silvia said to her, "Don't worry about being afraid. I will be holding up your arms for you."

It is not all up to us. Or any one of us. Nor is it all up to all of us together. God is with us. The Spirit of God is holding up the arms of those who hold up the arms, putting the song of the Lord on the harp strings and the voices of those who sing.

In a very touching exchange between my sisters, Peggy asked Mary to help her with how to pray as she tries to live with "the brain thing." Mary was close to tears at the request, at this strange turn in the road of life where Peggy, who had been the family leader for so long, now needed the wisdom Mary has gleaned from her long years of mental illness.

"You do the best you can," Mary replied simply, "with whatever effort you are able to manage at that moment. You pray however you can manage. And then you remind yourself that the Holy Spirit does the rest. What helps me the most, over and over, is the assurance that the Holy Spirit will do what we cannot. It is Romans 8:26-27."

She knew it by heart: "The Spirit…comes to help us in our weakness. For when we cannot choose words in order to pray properly, the Spirit … expresses our plea in a way that could never be put into words, and God who knows everything in our hearts knows perfectly well what [the Spirit] means" (JB).

That exchange has been like a star for me since then. It is not all up to us.

For Peggy, for Mary, for all of us, the Spirit will do what we cannot.

16

Easter Stories

A little mouse is in a castle dungeon in the hands of an old jailer who is giving him a chance to save himself by telling a story. The jailer says: "Stories are light. Light is precious in a world so dark. Begin at the beginning. Tell a story. Make some light.

> Kate DiCamillo,
> *The Tale of Despereaux*

These past months in our world have been times of hurricanes, earthquakes, and tsunami. Sometimes the seasons in our personal lives are like this: one storm after another brewing over the warm oceans of our circumstances. Stretches of time where challenge after crisis leave us worried, wearied, and wounded.

Like George on the first day of school, we have too much dark in our eyes.

In our private lives, and in our global human family so battered by the gales of war and terror, we have need of stories. Like the little mouse in the castle dungeon, we need to tell stories to make some light—and to save our lives. It is time to tell the Easter stories.

Fr. Demetrius Dumm writes that the Bible does not primarily contain teaching addressed to our intellect, as most other sacred literature does, but rather stories that invite us to trust.[1] Scripture helps us remember God's great acts of love and mercy, not as something that happened long ago, but as something in which we are participating right now. The stories of scripture help us name the stories of mercy in our present moment, the new acts in the eternal play of God's love.

There are stories I go back to in my own heart in times of storm and dark, stories from the Bible and stories that I have lived or heard about, stories that bring light.

There are three from the past year that have particularly touched me. Each in its way is hard to believe. Each one I have sometimes hesitated to tell in a talk I am giving because it seems so improbable, and I worry that people might feel discouraged that something like this has not happened in their own lives. But they do happen. They did happen. So I tell them again and again, the way the Jews keep telling the Exodus story.

Every year at Passover, Jewish people retell the story of God leading them out of slavery, not implying that God's people will always be miraculously spared from harm—for they know well the horror tales from the Babylonian Captivity to the Holocaust—but as an assurance of God's loving presence in events. The Exodus story is an archetype of the ways God ultimately delivers us from slavery and destruction. Retelling it builds a foundation of hope, a seasoned trust that God is with us in every event, giving life in ways we cannot see or may not understand.

I think we need to retell the archetypal stories in our own lives, not as predictors of constant miracles, but as bright illuminations of the central miracle that God brings all of us to Easter.

The first story is about my son Boo's wife, Caroline. She is one of the most tender people I have ever known, competent and lovely, a wonderful mother of their Hunter and Hannah.

Last fall she had a very frightening time. Chest pains and shortness of breath sent her to the doctor who ordered major heart tests. She was born with a heart defect and had open-heart surgery when she was twelve. The surgery was successful but extremely traumatic for her, with several complications from which she nearly died.

When her doctor reviewed the test results, he said that her bypass had closed. She needed an immediate cardiac catheterization to see exactly what the situation was—and possibly another open-heart surgery.

She was nearly paralyzed with fear, suddenly twelve years old again inside. They put her on some heavy heart medications that made her nearly nonfunctioning.

The day after the test results, I talked to her mother on the phone, both of us deeply concerned, pouring out our trepidations to each other. When I got off the phone, I was taut with worry.

I happened to glance out onto our balcony that overlooks the water. There, holding onto the railing, was a great osprey with a big fish in one of its claws. Looking right at me! I immediately thought of Caroline's favorite hymn, "On Eagle's Wings" . . . and remembered that the osprey is in the eagle family.

I just stared at the bird. I felt as if it were a messenger from God saying to me, "I will bear you up on eagle's wings. I will feed you." The osprey looked at me and I looked at it for ten full minutes. I finally made some kind of small movement, and he flew off.

The next day I was praying for Caroline at sunrise, looking out at the water and sky. The osprey circled, and then landed on the TV antenna on the roof of a house right below us. It stayed there an hour and a half! Again, just looking at me. Every time I would do something for awhile and then go back and look, it would still be there. It occurred to me that the TV antenna is the means through which we get the picture and hear the sound. "Let those who have eyes to see, see; let those who have ears to hear, hear,"[2] I said to myself.

While the osprey was sitting there, it began to rain—a drenching tropical downpour. It stayed right there. Shaking off the water once in a while, but not leaving. I felt as if God was saying to me: "In sun and storm, I am with you."

The next day was the catheterization procedure, an examination of the heart with some kind of tube/camera inserted through an artery in the groin. It was scheduled in Orlando for 9:00 a.m. I began to pray at dawn, and when I first got up, I saw the osprey on his favorite perch near the water. A few minutes later he was gone.

I kept praying and reading scripture and listening to music and holding Caroline in my heart. All the time I kept my eye out for the osprey, but did not see it again. I told myself that, of course, God's presence did not depend on the osprey . . . but I still kept looking for it.

No news at 10:00. No news at 11:00. I began to be really worried that they had taken her straight to surgery to open up her heart. I knew that in these procedures, they were set up to do so immediately, if necessary.

At 11:10 the osprey flew right by the balcony. Its wing came over the railing and dropped a feather on the balcony tiles!

A minute later the phone rang. It was Caroline's sister calling for Boo with the amazing news: When the doctor looked at the image from the catheter camera, he said, "Why, it looks brand new! Beautiful! Perfect! No blockage at all."

They had no explanation why the tests had shown the old bypass blocked. They told Caroline she could live a perfectly normal life with no medicines. An Easter story on eagle's wings!

I just shake my head remembering that morning. What are the chances? But what were the chances the Red Sea would part? That Sarah would conceive in her old age? That the blind would see, the lame would walk, the poor would have the good news preached to them? Most of all, what are the chances the tomb in a hillside outside Jerusalem would be found with the stone rolled back, empty, on the third day? The stories remind us that God is bringing all of us to Easter.

The second story is a tale from hurricane season. I mentioned earlier that Randy and Silvia sold our old family home to move out in the country to a trailer on a beautiful piece of land. A dirt road leads to it, off Route 66, an east/west county road that ends in Zolpho Springs, a tiny town with a log cabin of the first pioneers. Randy's land is filled with trees—huge pines, original old oaks. It is one of the few stretches in that area that was never cleared for orange groves or pasture.

In a hurricane, trailers must be evacuated. The destruction rate is very high for those slight structures. It was Randy and Silvia's tenth anniversary, and weeks before, I had reserved a room for them in a nice hotel in Sebring as a gift. The plan had been that we would keep the boys so Randy and Silvia could spend the weekend alone. Instead, the hotel room became the refuge for the entire family, a place to flee to from the trailer. The reservation was a huge stroke of luck because all inland hotels were jammed with people from the coast.

Watching the storm's path on our news channel, I was grateful beyond words that they were in that strong hotel. But I was also praying for their trailer. Everything they owned was in it, and they had no insurance. They had worked endlessly fixing it up and had turned it into a lovely little home. In horror I watched as the eye of the hurricane moved right through Zolpho Springs, the raging mass of wind and rain directly over their land.

When phone service was finally restored days later, I heard the story from Silvia. She told me how they had been praying, huddled together in the hotel room. The windows had bowed in so far, they looked as if the wind would break them—but they held. Water poured around the edges—but they held.

About an hour later, when the worst of the wind and rain had passed, Randy and Silvia found they could not stay in the hotel any longer. They had to know what had happened to their trailer. With the exhausted boys asleep in the back of the van, they made their way through the chaos. Power lines and phone poles were broken by the wayside. They steered around trees in the road. The closer they went down Route 66 to their dirt road, the worse was the damage. Great flattened barns and roofless houses were outlined by their headlights in the dark. Their road was nearly blocked by giant limbs; they had to circumvent their driveway to find a clearing to stop. Holding their breath, they shone the flashlight toward their home. Still standing! Roof intact! Windows all unbroken!

Carrying the boys, they made their way to the front door. There it all was just as they had left it: the couch with the green quilt folded on the back. The kitchen table. The new wood floor. The cross. The backpacks for the school year that had just started. Andrew's Elmo, Jacob's soccer trophy, George's small guitar.

A flash of lightning made them look out the back window, and they had a shocking revelation. A tornado had come right through the yard! Huge pine trees were snapped in half, giant oak trees were totally uprooted. But the trees had all fallen away from the trailer. The trailer was untouched. They held each other, praying silently, the miracle of life too big for words.

It made no difference that there was no power; they were home. They laid the boys in the king-sized bed and climbed in around them, all together safe.

As Silvia told the story, the antiphon from Jeremiah 29 that had been the lectionary's scripture passage on the morning of the hurricane came back to me: "The Lord says: my plans for you are peace and not disaster; when you call to me, I will listen to you, and I will bring you back to the place from which I exiled you."[3]

Through the years, as other kinds of storms break across our lives, we will tell ourselves this story, not assuming that we will go untouched, but reliving the grace of this event of mercy, trusting in the promise of ultimate peace and homecoming.

The final tale is from a dear friend of mine, Sr. Maureen Therese McGroddy, who codirects the School of Applied Theology sabbatical program at Berkeley. Nearly twenty years ago she was a counselor on the faculty of the international school that her community runs in Rome. There was a student whom I'll call Carmen who was very dear to Therese. Sometimes Carmen came to school with strange bruises and welts, and one day she confided to Therese that her stepfather was abusing her.

Therese spoke to the mother who was outraged and called the daughter a filthy liar. The stepfather was a very wealthy man, who Therese always suspected was connected with the Italian underworld. He was constantly seen with powerful people of all kinds in the worlds of film, politics, and business.

Not long after this Carmen ran away, and the father stormed the school demanding that they find her and return her to him. Therese had no idea where Carmen was. Eventually, she heard that the girl had been seen in the company of a man called Il Lupa, the Wolf, a drug dealer. Then some time later, that she had been seen along one of the Roman bridges where prostitutes solicited. Therese tried to find her but was never able to do so.

A week before Therese was leaving Rome permanently for the United States, she received a call from a nursing sister that the girl was in the ward of her hospital. Therese went right away, and the sister met her saying, "Carmen is dying. There is no place left in her veins to put a needle." The girl's poor arms were like sticks, filled with marks from shooting up heroin.

When Carmen opened her eyes and saw Therese, she turned her face to the wall, saying, "Oh, Sister, you should not have come. I am evil. You must hate me."

Therese held her and said, "Dear one, dear one, dear one, don't say that. You are precious and beautiful. I will always love you." She held Carmen until she fell asleep.

Decades have passed since then. Therese, long back in this country, had always been sure that Carmen had died soon after this last visit. It was several years ago that Therese first told me the tragic story, tearing up as she remembered.

In the summer she called with a different kind of tears to tell me she had gotten an e-mail from an address she did not recognize, from a doctor whom I will call Carmen Valenti. It was from the girl, now long a woman!

She had somehow recovered, escaped from her father and her life in Rome, come to New York where her mother's family lived, and gone back to school. She is now a psychiatrist who works full-time with troubled girls. She had just managed to track down Therese's e-mail address.

Therese read me the closing message from Carmen: "Sister, I have always longed to tell you: it was your love that saved me. Because of you, I could somehow trust God's love. Now I'm trying to pass that love on."

It is all about love. The Easter stories. The God who saves us.

Anything can happen. What the stories tell us is not that miracles will always happen, or even often happen, but that some kind of life will triumph over the many kinds of death. Nothing can separate us from Love.

"Stories are light. Light is precious in a world so dark. Begin at the beginning. Tell a story. Make some light."

Conclusion: Tender Mercies

That first week . . . was a consolation, a pure relief. The world will give you that once in a while, a brief time out; the boxing bell rings and you go to your corner, where somebody dabs mercy on your beat-up life.

Sue Monk Kidd,
The Secret Life of Bees

Life is so much harder than we expect. We run into walls, like George on the first day of school, because we have too much dark in our eyes. Each of us comes to the mystery of darkness in the unfolding of our unique story. My sister Peggy and the trouble with her brain. My sister Mary with her mental illness. Every human journey with its own chaos.

Once in a while, Sue Monk Kidd writes, "somebody dabs mercy on your beat-up life."

A term often used in scripture for the kindness of God is "tender mercies." I love that phrase for the experiences of goodness that I call light. Experiences of goodness that, when we receive them and remember them, undergo a kind of transformation, a photosynthesis into trust in Goodness itself that sustains our hope. We are given the grace to see the canvas of life as *chiaroscuro,* a beautiful interplay of shadow and light.

As the final edge of the hurricanes passed by our coast that fall, the osprey once again appeared, this time on our now-ruined dock, and sent its clear, wild call into the end of the day. It was Rosh Hashanah, the first day of the new year of the ancient Jewish calendar. According to oral tradition, this holy day marks the anniversary of the creation of the world. It is a day Jews ask for forgiveness, for a good year, for a long life. The great ram's horn, the horn of the animal that Abraham sacrificed in place of Isaac after the angel's intervening command (Gn 22:13), the *shofar,* is sounded. It is the day God is said to decide who will live and who will die.

Just as the sun was setting, my husband Howard's daughter, Laurie, called from a hospital in Georgia to say that she had given birth to Howard's first granddaughter. They had named the baby Sarah.

Sarah! The wife of Abraham, the one who laughed out loud when she was told she would bear a son in her old age and must have laughed till she could hardly stop crying when she heard that Isaac had been spared.

Filled with wonder for tiny Sarah, I looked out at the water and saw the retreating storm clouds backlit by the setting sun. Etched high above them was the sharp bright curve of the new moon. The new year for the Jews, from times before the written word, began with the new moon. For ancient people this was the moon most celebrated. It meant that light was born again in the darkness.

I am writing this book because, again and again in the sequence of my life's unfolding, there have been new moons, tender mercies, light born again in darkness.

I have learned from my sisters in their terrible struggles, and from so many beloved companions, how important it is to let in the light. To consciously focus on goodness, to reframe negativity, to reassure each other that struggle is nothing to be ashamed of. There is perfection in imperfection, and no way to learn to ride a bike without losing some skin. As Cohen wrote, "There is a crack in everything, that's how the light gets in."

We take our harps from the willow trees and play for each other the song of the Lord when we can. We offer up hardships and meet each other in kindness where it does not matter if we are the ones giving or the ones receiving. We are doing the work of *Tikkun Olam* as we sustain and restore the world. With us in it all, and doing what we cannot do, is the Spirit of God.

Still, sooner or later, we get frightened again of the dark, of storms of all sorts, of terror and war and diseases that tangle our brains. We get even more frightened for the ones we love than for ourselves.

A final story. It was before Christmas one year, at a time I was especially afraid for someone I love.

My children and all their children were gathering for supper, and I had come a little early to help set up. As soon as I got there, Andrew, who was two at the time, motioned me urgently into a corner of the living room to tell me something. (He is astoundingly verbal.) His huge, brown eyes were very serious under his fringe of fine red hair.

"Grandma! Guess what?"

"What, Andrew?"

"Monsters . . . not real." He looked around, and then he whispered, "Don't be scared, Grandma. Don't be scared."

Monsters. An image for a little child very much like a black hole into whose orbit our star can be pulled . . . out from under the blankets, away from our teddy bear, out of hearing of Mom and Dad.

Monsters. The strange haunting fears, the formless malicious energy, that threaten sometimes in the dark, that seem to be lurking in the closets of our hearts, the closets of the world.

"Grandma, guess what? Monsters . . . *not real*."

I gathered him up, holding him close, light pouring out from that utterly timeless message from the heart of Mystery itself.

"Monsters . . . not real." They do not have the ultimate power. They cannot lock us, or our world, away from love in the never-ending dark.

What is real is the power of love, freely given, poured out. Love, the antiparticle to all that is un-love. Love that was once dragged into the closet of a tomb on a hillside and then burst forth like a quasar on Easter morning.

In the chiaroscuro of our beat-up lives, the light shines in the darkness and the darkness will not overcome it.

"Don't be scared. It'll be all *raaht*."

Notes

1. Light and Life

1. "Where Does Your Faith Fit in the Cosmos? The Editors Interview Brian Swimme," *U.S. Catholic*, June 2002. This material is also in Swimme's book *The Hidden Heart of the Cosmos*. Maryknoll, NY: Orbis Books, 1996, pp. 38-44.
2. Reynolds Price, *Blue Calhoun*. New York: Scribner, 1992.

2. The Power of Negativity

1. Erma Bombeck, *If Life Is a Bowl of Cherries, What Am I Doing in the Pits?* New York: McGraw Hill, 1978.
2. This material about Candace Pert's research at Georgetown University can be found in her compelling book *Molecules of Emotion* (New York: Touchstone, 1999). Another resource with fascinating demonstrations of the effect of the positive and negative energy of thoughts is offered in the water studies of Japanese scientist Dr. Masuru Emoto. His book, *The Hidden Messages in Water* (Hillsboro, OR: Beyond Words Publishing, 2004), offers his high-speed photographic images of slides of frozen water. They show stunning examples of how crystals form or malform in water in response to messages such as love or gratitude, disdain or hate. Because our bodies are composed largely of water, this book speaks to the

impact of our thoughts on the health of our bodies and minds.

4. The Mixedness of Life

1. Pert, pp. 192-93.
2. Leonard Cohen, "Anthem" (from the album *Age of Aquarius*).
3. This arrangement of darkness and light is a theme throughout Kate DiCamillo's Newbery Medal Book *The Tale of Despereaux.* Cambridge, MA: Candlewick Press, 2003).
4. Jon Kabat-Zinn, *Full Catastrophe Living.* New York: Delacorte Press, 1990.

5. Titration

1. "Where Does Your Faith Fit in the Cosmos? The Editors Interview Brian Swimme," *U.S. Catholic,* June 2002.
2. Louise L. Hay, *You Can Heal Your Life.* Carlsbad, CA: Hay House, Inc., 1984, p. 150. The feature article of the January 17, 2005, issue of *Time* magazine, "The Science of Happiness," offers a collection of articles demonstrating the crucial impact of happiness on health, longevity, quality of life, safety, relationships, and productivity.

6. Dark Night of the Soul

1. "Spiritual Companions in the Dark Night" was a talk given at a conference of spiritual directors in June 2002 in Princeton, New Jersey.

7. Sources of Light

1. The news reports are from the Associated Press. The direct quotations are from a 1/12/05 report by Vijay Joshi published in the *Tampa Tribune.*

8. Laughter

1. These groups are described with a glorious picture on page A 26 in "The Science of Happiness" feature article mentioned above in the January 17, 2005, issue of *Time* magazine.
2. Rich Heffern, "Spirit in a World of Connection," *National Catholic Reporter*, May 2, 2003, p. 13.
3. Eugenie O'Neill, *Lazarus Laughed*, in the text as published by Boni & Liveright, 1927.

9. Light for Each Other

1. George M. Anderson, SJ, "Of Many Things," *America*, November 3, 2003.

10. Meeting in Kindness

1. Rachel Naomi Remen, M.D., *My Grandfather's Blessings*. New York: Riverhead Books, 2000, p. 7.
2. Remen, p. 6.

12. Light for Prayer

1. Much of this chapter appeared first as an article, "How to Refresh Your Prayer Life," in *Liguorian* magazine, January 2005.
2. Peter van Breemen, SJ, *The God Who Won't Let Go*. Notre Dame, IN: Ave Maria Press, 2001, p. 12.

13. Photosynthesis of Trust

1. Demetrius Dumm, OSB, *Praying the Scriptures*. Collegeville, MN: Liturgical Press, 2003, p. 44.
2. "Where Does Your Faith Fit in the Cosmos? The Editors Interview Brian Swimme," *U.S. Catholic*, June 2002. I was fascinated by what an incredible breakthrough photosynthesis was for the life of our planet. More of what Swimme said in the interview follows:

When the earliest life forms first came about ... the sun would activate chemical interactions in the oceans, which created a number of molecules, and these molecules were consumed by the life forms, but after a while, there was not enough food for all the life forms. The life forms would have died off if not for a mutation event that enabled life forms to actually capture sunlight. This is way back 3.5 billion years ago, and it is really a feat.

Light is moving at 186,000 miles a second and a life form has to capture a piece of it. But the even trickier part is that light comes in chunks called *photons*, and when you touch a photon to capture it, it disappears. Amazingly life forms fashioned a molecular net that, when it captures the light, actually transforms its shape and holds it until it needs energy, at which point it goes back to its original form. . . . photosynthesis."

3. Patricia H. Livingston, *This Blessed Mess*. Notre Dame, IN: Sorin Books, 2000, pp. 100-104.

4. Randy Livingston, the *Sebring News*.

5. Remen, pp. 2-3.

14. Offer It Up

1. Elizabeth Goudge, *The Heart of the Family*. London: Hodder & Stoughton, 1953, pp. 129 and 226.

2. This is actually how a PET Scan works in medical testing: positrons are injected into the patient in a glucose solution. Wherever there are unusual collections of electrons, which would be found in tumors or cancer sites, they attract the injected positrons. When they meet there are bursts of

light. It is these bursts of light that appear on the PET Scan screen and indicate to doctors where the abnormality is.

3. Barbara Fiand, SNDN, Holy Week Retreat, Franciscan Center, Tampa, FL, April 16-19, 2003. This material is also treated in her book *In the Stillness You Will Know* (New York: Crossroad Publishing Co, 2002).

4. Apostolic Letter *Salvifici Doloris* of Pope John Paul II on the Christian Meaning of Human Suffering, February 11, 1984, St. Peter's Rome, Sections 8, 24, 27. Available on the Internet.

5. *The HarperCollins Encyclopedia of Catholicism*, Richard P. McBrien, General Editor, San Francisco: HarperCollins, 1995, pp. 1089-1090

16. Easter Stories

1. Dumm, p. vii.

2. Matthew 11:15; 13:9, 16, 43; Mark 4:9, 23; Luke 8:8; 14:35.

3. Entrance Antiphon, Thirty-Third Sunday in Ordinary Time, from Jeremiah 29:11, 12, 14.

Bibliography

Anderson, George M. "Of Many Things," *America*, November 3, 2003.

Bombeck, Erma. *If Life Is a Bowl of Cherries, What Am I Doing in the Pits?* New York: McGraw Hill, 1978.

Chittister, Joan. *Wisdom Distilled from the Daily: Living the Rule of St. Benedict Today.* New York: Harper Collins Publishers, 1991.

Cooper, Susan. *The Dark Is Rising.* New York: Simon & Schuster, 1973.

DiCamillo, Kate. *The Tale of Despereaux: Being the Story of a Mouse, a Princess, Some Soup, and a Spool of Thread.* Cambridge, MA: Candlewick Press, 2003.

Dumm, Demetrius. *Cherish Christ Above All.* Mahwah, NJ: Paulist Press, 1996.

———. *Praying the Scriptures.* Collegeville, MN: Liturgical Press, 2003.

Emoto, Masuru. *The Hidden Messages in Water.* Hillsboro, OR: Beyond Words Publishing, 2004.

Fiand, Barbara. *In the Stillness You Will Know: Exploring the Paths of Our Ancient Belonging.* New York: Crossroad Publishing Co., 2002.

Goudge, Elizabeth. *The Heart of the Family.* London: Hodder & Stoughton, 1953.

Hay, Louise L. *You Can Heal Your Life.* Carlsbad, CA: Hay House, Inc., 1984.

Heffern, Rich. "Spirit in a World of Connection," *National Catholic Reporter*, May 2, 2003.

John Paul II. Apostolic Letter *Salvifici Doloris, On the Christian Meaning of Human Suffering*, February 11, 1984, St. Peter's Rome, Sections 8, 24, 27. Available on the Internet.

Kabat-Zinn, Jon. *Full Catastrophe Living: Using the Wisdom of Your Body and Mind to Face Stress, Pain, and Illness.* New York: Delacorte Press, 1990.

Kidd, Sue Monk. *The Secret Life of Bees.* New York: Viking Press, 2002.

Livingston, Patricia H. *This Blessed Mess: Finding Hope Amidst Life's Chaos.* Notre Dame, IN: Sorin Books, 2000.

Luke, Helen. *The Way of Woman: Awakening the Perennial Feminine.* New York: Doubleday, 1995.

O'Neill, Eugene G. *Lazarus Laughed (1925-1926): A Play for an Imaginative Theatre.* New York: Boni and Liveright, 1927.

Pert, Candace B. *Molecules of Emotion: The Science Behind Mind-Body Medicine.* New York: Touchstone, 1999.

Price, Reynolds. *Blue Calhoun.* New York: Scribner, 1992.

Remen, Rachel Naomi, M.D. *My Grandfather's Blessings: Stories of Strength, Refuge, and Belonging.* New York: Riverhead Books, 2000.

Rowling, J. K. *Harry Potter and the Prisoner of Azkaban.* London: Bloomsbury Publishing, 1999.

"The Science of Happiness," *Time*, January 17, 2005.

Swimme, Brian. *The Hidden Heart of the Cosmos.* Maryknoll, NY: Orbis Books, 1996.

van Breemen, Peter. *The God Who Won't Let Go.* Notre Dame, IN: Ave Maria Press, 2001.

"Where Does Your Faith Fit in the Cosmos? The Editors Interview Brian Swimme," *U.S. Catholic*, June 2002.

PATRICIA LIVINGSTON, a sought-after public speaker, inspires audiences with down-to-earth tales of everyday living. Besides leading workshops, retreats, and seminars throughout the United States and abroad, Livingston is an award-winning writer whose work has been featured in *Praying, St. Anthony Messenger, Studies in Formative Spirituality,* and *U.S. Catholic.* In 1990, Livingston was awarded the U.S. Catholic Award for furthering the cause of women in the Catholic Church. Her previous books, *Lessons of the Heart* and *This Blessed Mess,* provide encouragement in the face of life's hectic, stress-filled demands. Livingston lives with her husband, Howard Gordon, in Tampa, Florida.

CELEBRATING THE RHYTHMS OF LIFE

THIS BLESSED MESS
Finding Hope Amidst Life's Chaos
Patricia H. Livingston

Offering hope and encouragement in the face of life's chaos, Pat Livingston's good humored stories assure us that in the midst of all the "craziness" we can discover, as she did, the seeds of creativity and hope.

ISBN: 1-893732-15-0 / 144 pages / $12.95
Sorin Books

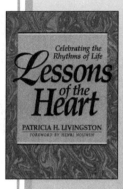

LESSONS OF THE HEART
Celebrating the Rhythms of Life
Patricia H. Livingston

A warm and compelling book that enables readers to see themselves with fresh tenderness. It offers hope and encouragement in the face of the hectic stress-filled demands of contemporary life.

ISBN: 0-87793-486-X / 128 pages / $8.95
Ave Maria Press

SLOW DOWN
Five-Minute Meditations to De-Stress Your Days
Joseph M. Champlin

These 101 spiritual messages allow people everywhere to reduce the stress that results from our never-slow-down days. Each message is accompanied by a spiritual suggestion for reflection and a prayer taken from the Psalms.

ISBN: 1-893732-78-9 / 208 pages / $9.95
Sorin Books

Available at your bookstore, online retailers, or from **ave maria press** at
www.avemariapress.com or 1-800-282-1865. Prices and availablity subject to change.

Keycode: FØTØ1Ø6ØØØØ